BOOKS BY ELGIN CIAMPI

The Underwater Guide to Marine Life *(with Carleton Ray)*

Photography Under Water

The Skin Diver

Those Other People the Porpoises

BOOKS BY ROBERT H. BOYLE

Sport, Mirror of American Life

The Water Hustlers *(with John Graves and T. H. Watkins)*

The Hudson River, A Natural and Unnatural History

The Fly-Tyer's Almanac *(edited with Dave Whitlock)*

The Second Fly-Tyer's Almanac *(edited with Dave Whitlock)*

Malignant Neglect *(with the Environmental Defense Fund)*

BASS

Text by Robert H. Boyle

Photographs by Elgin Ciampi

W. W. Norton & Company

New York / London

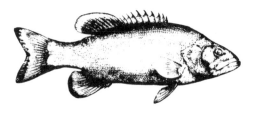

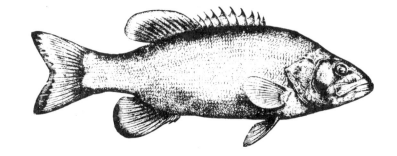

BASS

*First published, 1980, in the United States by W.W. Norton
& Company, Inc., New York. Published simultaneously in
Canada by George J. McLeod Limited, Toronto.
All rights reserved under International and Pan-American
Copyright Conventions. Printed and bound by Dai Nippon
Printing Co., Ltd., Tokyo, Japan.
First Edition
Design by Cynthia Krupat
Library of Congress Cataloging in Publication Data
Boyle, Robert H
Bass.
Bibliography: p.
Includes index.
1. Largemouth bass fishing. 2. Largemouth bass.
3. Bass fishing. I. Ciampi, Elgin. II. Title.
SH681.B69 1980   799.1' 758   80–13657
ISBN 0–393–01379–0*

We are grateful to the following for permission to reprint portions of
this work based on or excerpted from: *Sports Illustrated,* "The Moment
They Hit the Lure," July 24, 1961; "This Is the Fish You Can't Catch
Too Many Of," by Robert H. Boyle, August 19, 1963; and "The Man's
Hooked on Plugs," by Robert H. Boyle, July 14, 1975. Cranbrook
Institute of Science, Bulletin 10, *The Small-Mouthed Bass,* by Carl L.
Hubbs and Reeve M. Bailey. Van Nostrand Reinhold Company,
Management of Lakes and Ponds, by George W. Bennett,
2nd edition, 1971.
R.H.B. / E.C.

1 2 3 4 5 6 7 8 9 0

To Renée and Kathryn,

and to the memory of the late George W. Bennett

for his pioneering studies on largemouth bass

and his concern for the natural world

Contents

Preface

This book was written to give fishermen, naturalists, or anyone who is curious about life beneath the water insight into the life history and ecology of the largemouth bass, the most sought-after freshwater game fish in the United States. Almost all the color photographs were taken in the wild, and we would like to thank Florida Silver Springs, the Florida Game and Fresh Water Commission, and the Shedd Aquarium of Chicago for their cooperation.

We would also like to thank Drs. James Atz and C. Lavett Smith of the American Museum of Natural History for their assistance, offered, as always, with generosity and enthusiasm. In addition, we would like to thank Dr. Dominick J. Pirone of Manhattan College, Dr. Alfred W. Eipper, now retired from the U.S. Fish and Wildlife Service, Arthur Brawley of Sports Illustrated, *Arthur Glowka of Stamford, Connecticut, the ubiquitous Seth Rosenbaum of Queens, New York, and Dr. R. Weldon Larimore of the Illinois Natural History Survey. We also owe a great debt to the late Dr. George W. Bennett of the survey.*

Finally, we would like to thank George Brockway and Starling Lawrence of W. W. Norton & Company for their patience. Banquo's ghost is at last laid to rest.

Robert H. Boyle / Elgin Ciampi

BASS

1/
The
Background
of Bass

The largemouth bass, *Micropterus salmoides*, is the most popular game fish in the United States. Present in every state except Alaska, the largemouth can live in brackish water sloughs, freshwater ponds and lakes, and slow-moving rivers. Feeding on a diet of crustacea, insects, other fishes, amphibians, and even small birds and mammals on occasion, the largemouth has been called close to the perfect all-around predator. To many of America's sixty million anglers the largemouth has no peer. As biologist Brian Curtis once wrote, "His character embodies traits which we like to think of as typically American: adaptability, gameness, individuality."

Along with the smallmouth and other so-called black basses, the largemouth is a member of the sunfish family, the Centrarchidae. The family is so named because of the development of the spines in the anal fin. The Centrarchidae are "advanced" fishes, a product of long evolutionary development that began during the Ordovician period some 400 million years ago when the first fish-like vertebrates appeared.

In the Triassic period of 200 million years ago, the herring-like Pholidophoriformes appeared. Approximately 100 million years after that, the Clupeiformes evolved. The first great order of modern bony fishes, the Clupeiformes of the present day include shad and herrings. Offshoots of the Clupeiformes begat the Beryciformes, the first spiny-rayed fishes, ancestors of the Perciformes, perch-like fishes, which appeared perhaps sixty million years ago. Evolutionary development was then very rapid. The Perciformes compose the largest order of fishes in the world today, numbering some 7500 species, a figure that approaches the number of species of birds in the world. The suborder Percoidei alone includes the families Centrarchidae, Percidae (perches, walleyes, and darters), Sciaenidae (drums), Centropomidae (snooks), Carangidae (jacks, scads, and pompanos), Pomatomidae (bluefish), and Serranidae (sea basses). According to studies conducted by Carl L. Hubbs and Reeve M. Bailey of the University of Michigan, the Centrarchidae are distinct from other families because of the following combination of taxonomic features:

The pelvic or ventral fins are thoracic in position. That is, the pair of fins on the belly are below or slightly behind the pectoral fins, which are inserted on the sides of the body just behind the gill covers.

The pelvic fins each have one spine and five branched rays.

The anal fin, the single fin on the lower side of the fish between the anus and tail fin, has three to eight spines, rarely two.

The forward portion of the dorsal fin has from five to fourteen spines joined by a membrane, and this spiny portion is connected with the soft rays behind, although in the largemouth bass the dorsal is almost divided.

The body and cheeks are covered with ctenoid scales, but the top of the head lacks scales. Ctenoid scales are those which are toothed rather than smooth on the edge.

The pseudobranchiae or accessory gills are concealed by a membrane. By contrast, they are exposed in the Serranidae, the sea bass family.

There are twenty-seven to thirty-three vertebrae, and all but one to three pairs of ribs are attached to the vertebrae. (This is a point to remember when filleting.)

There is no subocular shelf, a small plate of bone, beneath the eye. By contrast, the sea bass possess a subocular shelf.

In addition, the sunfishes also share some common characteristics of behavior, notably in breeding. With the exception of the Sacramento perch (*Archoplites interruptus*), the males of all the species make a nest and guard the eggs.

The sunfish family is now divided into three subfamilies, as illustrated on page 17 in the family tree or "theoretical phyologeny." For example, the crappies are placed in the subfamily Centrarchinae because of their bone and fin structure. They are considered among the most advanced of the sunfish because, among other differences, of the great development of their anal fin. By contrast, the black basses, which are "generalized" and not specialized like the crappies, belong to the subfamily Lepominae where they branch off to form a tribe of their own, the Micropterini.

The Centrarchidae are native to North America. In fact, with the sole exception of the Sacramento perch all were originally found east of the Rocky Mountains. "The sunfish family was unknown to the Europeans before they came to

The Centrarchid Family Tree

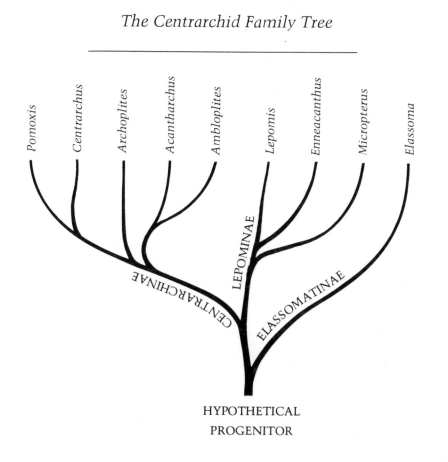

HYPOTHETICAL
PROGENITOR

(Redrawn and adapted from "Evolution of the Dorsal-Fin Supports of Percoid Fishes," by C. Lavett Smith and Reeve M. Bailey, Papers of the Michigan Academy of Science, Arts, and Letters, Vol. 46, 1961.)

America," Erhard Rostlund writes in *Freshwater Fish and Fishing in Native North America*, "and one might expect that these strange new fishes would have aroused curiosity and inspired many comments in the early narratives, but they did not, and I have no explanation for the silence."

One of the few noteworthy observations on bass was made in the 1760s by John Bartram, botanist for King George III, and his son William, who noted how the Seminole Indians of Florida bobbed for bass with deer-hair lures, the forerunner of the present-day fisherman's bug.

Even in the scientific literature of the nineteenth century, starting in 1802 when the comte de Lacépède at the Jardins des Plantes in Paris first described the smallmouth and largemouth bass sent to him, there was confusion. The smallmouth Lacépède received had a deformed dorsal fin, and he gave the species the scientific name of *Micropterus dolomieu*. *Micropterus* means "little fin" while the specific epithet *dolomieu* was given in honor of D. G. Dolomieu, a geologist who discovered the mineral dolomite. Failing to recognize that the largemouth bass belonged to the same genus as the smallmouth, Lacépède named it *Labrus salmoides*, which means "trout-like wrasse." In the years that followed, various other taxonomists gave the black bass still more generic names, such as *Calliurus, Aplites, Lepomis, Nemocampsis, Dioplites, Aplesion, Huro,* and *Grystes.*

In 1896 David Starr Jordan and Barton W. Evermann reviewed all previous research in their monumental work *The Fishes of North and Middle America*, and called the large-

mouth *Micropterus salmoides* and the smallmouth *Micropterus dolomieu* (now spelled with an *i* at the end). Jordan and Evermann recognized only these two species of black bass, but taxonomists now agree that there are six species of bass, and possibly a seventh. They are the largemouth, smallmouth, spotted, redeye, Suwannee, Guadalupe, and the question-mark shoal bass. There are two largemouth subspecies, the common or northern largemouth *Micropterus salmoides salmoides*, and the Florida largemouth *Micropterus salmoides floridanus*.

Originally the northern largemouth ranged in parts of southern Canada and the Great Lakes, the entire Mississippi Valley, in the south from Texas (and possibly northeastern New Mexico) east to northern Florida, and up the Atlantic coastal plain to North Carolina. It was absent from the Atlantic drainage of the northeastern United States. The usual habitat was weedy lakes and ponds, sluggish streams, and backwaters. Maximum size is about twelve pounds.

The Florida largemouth was not recognized as a subspecies until 1949 when Reeve M. Bailey and Carl L. Hubbs of the University of Michigan published a paper, "The Black Basses (*Micropterus*) of Florida, with Description of a New Species," designating it as such. Defining its native range is difficult because, as Bailey and Hubbs noted, "a natural orderly situation has been complicated by the extensive stocking of northern *salmoides*" which can interbreed with the Florida largemouth. In fact, to the north and west of its present range the Florida largemouth "intergrades" with the northern largemouth, and there is marked intergradation of fish along U.S. Highway 1, the possible route of introduction by man of the northern largemouth. According to Bailey and Hubbs, the Florida largemouth is to be found throughout Florida "northward in the east to the mouth of the St. John's River system." In all likelihood the Florida largemouth evolved as a subspecies during glacial times when the Florida peninsula was partially or completely cut off from the rest of North America.

The Florida and northern largemouths look very much alike, but there are a few key differences. One discernible difference is in scales, as enumerated in the table (adapted from Bailey and Hubbs).

SCALE DIFFERENCES IN NORTHERN AND FLORIDA LARGEMOUTHS

Criterion	Northern largemouth (M. s. salmoides)	Florida largemouth (M. s. floridanus)
Number of scale rows above lateral line	Usually 7 or 8	Usually 8 or 9
Number of scale rows below lateral line	Usually 14–17	Usually 17 or 18
Number of scales along lateral line	Usually 59–67	Usually 69–73
Number of scale rows around the caudal peduncle	Usually 26–28	Usually 28–31

Another important difference is that the Florida largemouth attains a larger size, occasionally reaching twenty pounds or more. In their paper Bailey and Hubbs noted that "it seemed probable that the large growth potential has in part a genetic basis." There were biologists who disagreed with this; they insisted that the Florida largemouth grew bigger because it lived in a rich, balmy environment where it could feed all year round. But Bailey and Hubbs were proven correct in somewhat unusual fashion. One day in the fall of 1958, Ray Boone, the first baseman for the Detroit Tigers, was fishing with Orville P. Ball, a biologist who was then superintendent of the reservoir lakes in San Diego, California. Boone allowed that he could hardly wait for spring training to begin so he could fish for the huge bass in Florida. Then Boone said, "Orville, why can't you get some of those big Florida bass out here?"

Ball did. In the spring of 1959 he arranged for the stocking of 20,400 pure-strain Florida largemouth fry in specially treated reservoir lakes. The early growth rate was not impressive, and one California biologist anounced that "all indications are…that the environment and not heredity is the important factor in maximum size and growth rate of the Florida largemouth bass." He was wrong by a wide margin, but it took until 1969, ten years after the stocking, to show it. That year a fisherman took a fifteen-pound four-ounce fish from Lake Miramar and in 1972 a fisherman took a seventeen-pound fourteen-ounce bass from Lake Murray. In 1973 Dave Zimmerlee of San Diego caught a twenty-pound fifteen-ounce fish in Lake Miramar, and there is speculation that a fish topping the world-record mark of twenty-two pounds four ounces, set in 1932 by George Perry in Montgomery Lake, Georgia, will come out of one of the San Diego lakes.

The smallmouth bass (*Micropterus dolomieui dolomieui*) is on a different branch of the family tree. Before its introduction by man elsewhere, it ranged from Québec, Ontario, and northern Minnesota south to Oklahoma and the Tennessee River system. Primarily a fish of cool streams and deep rocky lakes, the world-record smallmouth is an eleven-pound fifteen-ounce fish caught by David Hayes in Dale Hollow Reservoir, Kentucky, in 1955.

No angler should have difficulty telling a smallmouth from a largemouth. The most obvious point of difference is the mouth—the mouth of the largemouth extends behind the rear of the eye, while that of the smallmouth does not. Fred Mather, a pioneer American pisciculturist, succinctly noted other differences between the two in this bit of doggerel:

> *The little-mouth has little scales,*
> *There's red in his handsome eye;*
> *The scales extend on his vertical fins,*
> *And his forehead is round and high.*

> *His forehead is full and high, my boys,*
> *And he sleeps the winter through;*

> *He likes the rocks in the summertime,*
> Micropterus dolomieu.

> *The big-mouth has the biggest scales,*
> *And a pit scooped in his head;*
> *His mouth is cut beyond his eye,*
> *In which is nary a red.*

> *In his eye is nary a red, my boys,*
> *But keen and well he sees;*
> *He has a dark stripe on his side,*
> Micropterus salmoides.

In 1940 Hubbs and Bailey, in "A Revision of the Black Basses," described and named a new subspecies of smallmouth, the Neosho smallmouth, *M. d. velox*, sometimes referred to as the Ozark smallmouth because it is found in mountain streams in Arkansas, Missouri, and Oklahoma. More slender in form than the common smallmouth, the Neosho smallmouth also has a projecting lower jaw so that the teeth are visible from above. The name *velox* ("swift") refers to its body form and reputation for gameness. Hubbs, who died recently, recognized *velox* as a subspecies, but Bailey no longer does.

The spotted bass or Kentucky bass is divided into three subspecies. The most prominent is the northern spotted bass, *M. punctlatus punctlatus*, the most common bass found in the upper Ohio River and its tributaries. It now ranges into the south from Georgia to Texas. The two other subspecies are confined in range; *M. p. henshalli*, known as the Alabama spotted bass, is centered on Alabama, Mississippi, and Georgia, while *M. p. wichitae*, the Wichita spotted bass, is found in the Wichita Mountains of Oklahoma. The world record is an Alabama spotted bass of eight pounds ten and a half ounces, caught in Lewis Smith Lake, Alabama, by Billy Henderson in 1972.

The redeye bass, *M. coosae*, is native to Alabama, Georgia, and Florida. Its specific name comes from the Coosa River in Georgia. The redeye has been called the brook trout of the black basses since it occupies a stream habitat and often feeds on surface insects. The species was first described by Hubbs and Bailey in their 1940 revision, and in a note accompanying specimens sent to them from Lake Auburn, Alabama, H. S. Swingle wrote, "Highly regarded by local fishermen because of their gameness. Maximum recorded weight, 2 pounds. A stream fish, it apparently cannot reproduce in a pond; or if it reproduces the spawn die. The young after reaching a length of several inches can stand pond water and grow rapidly. Flesh of good quality, somewhat drier than the large-mouthed bass. Can be caught on worms, artificial lures, or live minnows." The record redeye, six pounds one-half ounce, was caught in Hallawakee Creek, Alabama, by Thomas Sharpe in 1967, but it may have been a "shoal" bass.

The Suwannee bass, *M. notius*, was recognized as a "strikingly distinct species" by Bailey and Hubbs in 1949 in "The

Black Basses of Florida." They wrote, "The bright blue on the lower anterior parts in life seems to be unique for the genus." The original specimens came from Ichtucknee Springs, a tributary of the Santa Fe River in northern Florida. The fish has since been taken from several streams in the area, notably the Suwannee River from which it draws its common name. The Suwannee bass is a small fish; the largest specimen Bailey and Hubbs examined was a mature male late in its fourth summer of life with a total length of only 10.6 inches.

The Guadalupe bass, *M. treculi*, has so far been found only in streams of the Edwards Plateau in central Texas. Small in size—a large one would be ten inches—the Guadalupe bass feeds primarily on aquatic insects.

The question-mark shoal bass, recently recognized as a species by John S. Ramsey of Auburn University, is found in the Chipola River in Florida and in the Chattahoochee, Chestatee, and Flint Rivers in Georgia. The species has yet to be described and given a scientific name.

No matter what scientific names bass were called, early nineteenth-century anglers applied their own. To New Yorkers, largemouths were known as "Oswego bass," while smallmouths were called "black bass." By whatever name, bass were not as esteemed as trout and salmon, for American angling stemmed from the British tradition which held trout and salmon the be-all and end-all and all other species as "coarse fish." In the south, bass were popularly known as

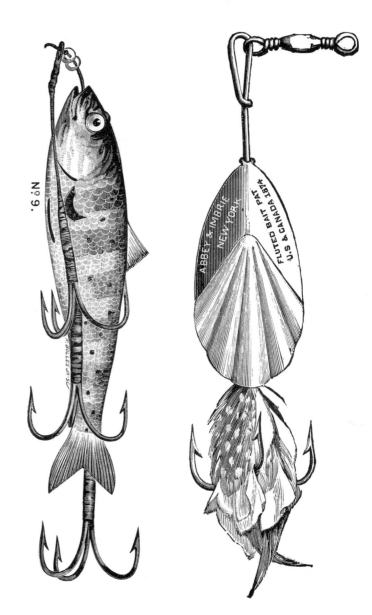

"trout" or "green trout," and in 1831 the editor of the *Turf Register* in Baltimore protested against the southern bass fisherman calling himself a "trout fisher." Although the editor noted that bass, largemouths presumably, sometimes reached ten or fifteen pounds, "there is no comparison, none at all, between sitting with your rod in a shallop, in one of the low, marshy lagoons of the south, surrounded by huge alligators sunning themselves lazily upon the blackened logs that float upon the turbid water, whose sluggish surface is not infrequently rippled by the darting of the deadly moccasin hissing past you—and treading the verdant banks of some beautiful, rippling brook in New England; gurgling and leaping in its living course to the ocean, with its cool retreat for its watery tenant [the brook trout]...."

This piscatorial snobbery persisted. Kit Clarke, a trout enthusiast, wrote some decades later, "Although giving the bass full credit for his great merit I am wearied of reading or listening to comparisons between the species; they seem to me much like an effort to compare the brilliancy of a diamond with that of a red brick. The black bass is an honor to the finny nation, but he should never be compared to the brook trout. The one is a thing of beauty and a joy forever, the other is a blackguard and a tough forever."

But the basses, largemouth and smallmouth, were finding favor. They gained entry to the Hudson River with the completion of the Erie Canal in 1825 and were soon stocked in ponds and lakes in the watershed to provide sport. In 1850, Samuel Tisdale of East Wareham, Massachusetts, brought twenty-seven bass, presumably smallmouths, from Saratoga Lake in New York and stocked them in Flax Pond near his home. From there bass were taken to stock twenty other nearby ponds, and from there they were eventually taken again for waters elsewhere in Massachusetts, Connecticut and New Hampshire. In 1865, H. R. Agnel of West Point, New York, wrote Thaddeus Norris, the author of *The American Angler's Book* and the father of angling in this country, that in 1859 he had paid ninety dollars to have sixty-one bass, all weighing more than a pound and a half, brought downstate from Saratoga Lake for stocking in Wood Lake in the Hudson Highlands. The bass settled in nicely, and Agnel reported they "now take the spoon readily, rise freely at a fly, and are often caught still-fishing with minnow or grasshopper." Not content with stocking Wood Lake, Agnel gave away bass "of the middle size" to anyone wishing to stock lakes or ponds in the area, and as a result, "many ponds and small lakes are now stocked."

In 1869, officials of the state of Maine and the Oquossoc Angling Association procured "a quantity of black bass" from Newburgh on the Hudson, for placement in various waters. The bass were soon reported "to have increased largely in numbers." Nowadays Maine is celebrated for its excellent smallmouth bass fishing.

Further south, other enthusiasts spread the smallmouth bass. In 1853, Gen. W. W. Shriver of Wheeling, West Virginia, "thinking the Potomac River admirably suited to the cultivation of the bass," took some twenty smallmouths from the Ohio River, placed them in the water tank of a locomotive of the Baltimore and Ohio Railroad, and released them into the basin of the Chesapeake & Ohio Canal at Cumberland, Maryland, "from which they had free egress to the Potomac River and its tributaries."

Starting in the 1870s, thanks to the completion of the transcontinental railroad and advances in fish culture, numerous species of fish, including the largemouth and smallmouth bass, were stocked in California and other parts of the West. Indeed, in short order California waters became "Atlanticized" with fish species from the East. Given ecological hindsight, such stockings were unwise because new species, "exotics," often disrupt native ecosystems, as witness the witless introduction of carp from Europe to American waters during the same period. While feeding on the bottom, carp roil the water, making it difficult for game fish, such as bass, which mainly feed by sight, to see their prey or hatch their eggs.

In the 1870s, 1880s, and 1890s, the great "fish transplant" craze hit the country. The first request from California authorities for fish came in 1871. The Californians were fearful that immigrant Chinese, who had come over to work on the railroad and who were very fond of fish, would seine the Sacramento River clean, and so that very same year 12,000 young shad from the Hudson River were carried west by train in four eight-gallon milk cans and dumped into the Sacramento. That was just the start. In 1873, for example, Livingston Stone of the U.S. Fish Commission set out for California with a special railroad aquarium car containing a veritable Noah's ark of fishes from the East, including 60 black bass (species not given) and 150 yellow perch from the vicinity of Lake Champlain, 1500 "saltwater" eels from Martha's Vineyard, 40,000 "freshwater" eels from the Hudson River (actually the freshwater and saltwater eels were the same species, but no one knew it then), 20,000 shad eggs and young from the Hudson, 1000 brook trout from New Hampshire, and 162 lobsters and a barrel of oysters from Woods Hole and Massachusetts Bays. Alas, after passing through Omaha the train crashed into the Elk Horn River and the whole carload was lost. But no matter, for new trains carried new fish west. In fact, California and Oregon owe their striped bass populations to 435 small stripers taken from the Shrewsbury and Navesink Rivers in northern New Jersey and planted in the San Francisco Bay area in 1879 and 1881.

By the 1890s, largemouth and smallmouth bass had been stocked every which way, and a report of the U.S. Commission of Fish and Fisheries noted, "This movement has not met with universal approval for by the ill-advised enthusiasm of some of its advocates, a number of trout streams have been destroyed, and complaints are heard that the fisheries of certain rivers have been injured by them."

With the surge of settlement across the Appalachians, the Middle West, and the Great Plains, the largemouth bass, whether native or stocked, gained new and often inventive enthusiasts. As early as 1810, George Snyder of Paris, Ken-

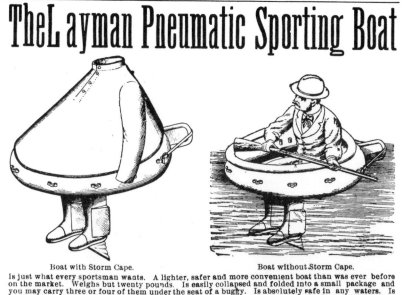

TheLayman Pneumatic Sporting Boat

Boat with Storm Cape.   Boat without Storm Cape.

Is just what every sportsman wants. A lighter, safer and more convenient boat than was ever before on the market. Weighs but twenty pounds. Is easily collapsed and folded into a small package and you may carry three or four of them under the seat of a buggy. Is absolutely safe in any waters. Is propelled by the feet, thus leaving the hands free to use gun or rod. Is made in four compartments of the best rubb r duck cloth; has loops for erecting a blind to shield you from the game; is quickly inflated, and in every way a success. Price $26.50 for men's sizes, weight 15 pounds; for boys' boats $22. Storm capes from $3 to $5. Send cash with orders to

AMERICAN RUBBER BOAT CO.,
Send for circulars.   487 Broadway, New York.

tucky, the president of the Bourbon County Angling Club, made the best multiplying reel in the world, and later in the century James Heddon of Dowagiac, Michigan, whittled the first commercial wooden plug. Cincinnati was the home of a physician, Dr. James A. Henshall, who wrote *The Book of the Black Bass.* The book was first published in 1881 and underwent numerous editions and printings in the course of the next fifty years, and it became the bible for the growing army of the faithful. Henshall, now the acknowledged father of black bass fishing in this country, announced that it was "inevitable" that the black bass would become "the leading game-fish of America," and he stirred controversy with his flat declaration that the black bass is "*inch* for *inch,* and *pound* for *pound,* the gamest fish that swims." There are those who contend that Henshall meant the smallmouth, but he himself wrote, "I am of the opinion that the large-mouth bass, all things being equal, displays as much pluck and exhibits as untiring fighting qualities as its small-mouth cousin."

Still another midwesterner who later did his part was Sen. Harry B. Hawes of Missouri, who in 1926 got a federal law, actually known as the Black Bass Act, passed to prevent interstate shipment of bass for commercial purposes where there was a state prohibition against it. The act is still on the books; in fact, it was updated and amended in 1969. Hawes was a man of some prescience. In his book *My Friend, the Black Bass,* published in 1930, he wrote of pollution, "It menaces human life as well as fish life."

The Middle West was the heart of largemouth bass fishing. One of the most celebrated fisheries was on the Illinois River, a major tributary of the Mississippi. As far back as 1673 when the French explored the region, the Illinois and its wildlife excited comment. "We have seen nothing like this river that we enter," wrote the French Jesuit Père Marquette. Long after he wrote that the rich Illinois remained a marvel. In the 1890s, bass fishermen and duck hunters took trains to Havana, Illinois, for a day's angling or shooting on the river with its lush aquatic plants and stands of pecans and pin oaks. Indeed, largemouth bass were so abundant that they were fished commercially with cane poles and shipped to market. In 1899 the black bass fisheries of the entire state, consisting almost entirely of largemouth bass, amounted to more than 120,000 pounds. Of this, the Illinois River alone accounted for 102,000 pounds.

The keys to the productivity of the Illinois were a couple of natural factors that had been at work since glacial times. Endowed with an unusually wide valley carved by the ice sheets, the Illinois built up natural levees with rich deposits of silt. In the spring the normally sluggish river flooded and water surged over the levees, creating large bottomland lakes. Bass and other fishes moved into these lakes, greatly extending their spawning grounds and food supply. The glories of the Illinois prompted Stephen A. Forbes of the Illinois Natural History Survey, a scientist who did much to found the science of ecology, to establish a field station at Havana to study "the effect on the aquatic plant and animal life of a

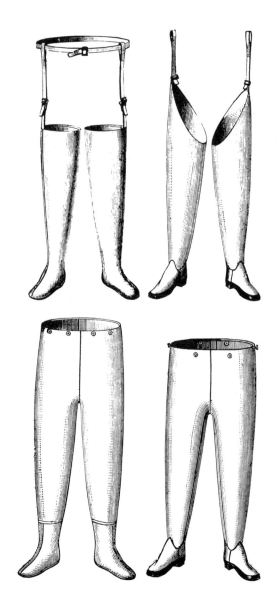

region produced by the periodic overflow and gradual recession of the waters of great rivers." Although the Illinois eventually became the "most studied" river in the world, it began to suffer from devastating abuse, first from sewage dumped in by the city of Chicago, and then by the drainage of some 400,000 acres of bottomland lakes for agriculture. Chronic pollution, increases in turbidity and sedimentation, and a decrease in aquatic vegetation have reduced the once-rich fishery to a ghost of its former size. Because of pollution, the main surviving fish species, the introduced carp, often exhibits a bone abnormality known as "knothead."

Even more widespread devastation was occurring in the trout country of the East and upper Middle West as the result of rapacious logging and the consequent silting of streams, the increase in water temperature from loss of cover, and the construction of dams.

Trout were unable to cope with such conditions, and often bass replaced them. As early as 1879, three years before Henshall's book appeared, Charles Hallock, the founder and editor of *Forest and Stream*, could foresee the future, pessimistic as it was for him:

No doubt the Bass is the appointed successor of the trout; but not through heritage, nor selection, nor by interloping, but by foreordination. Truly, it is sad to contemplate, in the not distant future, the extinction of a beautiful race of creatures, whose attributes have been sung by all the poets; but we regard the inevitable with the same calm philosophy with which the astronomer watches the burning out of a world, knowing that it will be succeeded by a new creation.

As we behold the soft vari-tinted flush of the trout disappear in the eventide, behold the sparkle of the coming Bass as he leaps in the morning of his glory! We hardly know which to admire the most—the velvet livery and the charming graces of the departing courtier, or the flash of the armor-plates of the advancing warrior. The Bass will unquestionably prove himself a worthy substitute for his predecessor, and a candidate for a full legacy of honors.

In the nineteenth century and continuing into the twentieth, enthusiasm arose for stocking bass abroad. In Europe, largemouth bass are to be found in France, Italy, Portugal, and Spain, and in limited quantities in Austria, Czechoslovakia, Great Britain, Switzerland, and the Soviet Union. The largemouth has also found a home in Mexico and Central America, parts of the Caribbean (notably Cuba, famed for the large fish of Treasure Lake, and Puerto Rico), and Brazil. The largemouth is also found in a number of African countries, including Botswana, Kenya, Lesotho, the Malagasy Republic, Morocco, Rhodesia, the Union of South Africa, Swaziland, Tanzania, and Uganda. Lake Naivasha, a seventy-square-mile lake 6000 feet high in Kenya, has been the source of some spectacular fishing, the outgrowth of a planting of fifty-six fingerlings in 1929. The lake had only one indigenous fish, a tiny cyprinodont, *Haplochilichthys antinorii*, which thrived by the millions. By 1931, bass up to four pounds were reported in the shallow lake, and by 1933 an angler did not consider it unusual to bag eighty largemouth over a weekend. Interestingly, by 1935 the tiny native minnow had practically disappeared and the bass had turned to feeding on the Naivasha clawed toad (*Xenopus*), small tilapia that had been stocked, and aquatic insects, principally dragonfly larvae.

Smallmouth have had far less success becoming established abroad. They are to be found in the Union of South Africa and in limited numbers in Belgium, Sweden, Hong Kong, and Vietnam. The spotted bass is to be found in South Africa and Rhodesia, and the redeye in the Jayuga River of Puerto Rico.

As might be expected, stocking and other early attempts at managing bass were based on assumptions lacking scientific foundation. In 1914 and 1915, Lewis L. Dyche of Kansas and George C. Embody of Cornell University published on fishery ponds. Dyche advocated stocking bass with crappies and sunfish, while Embody recommended that ponds be stocked with an assortment of species, the forage fish first. Embody's recommendations were not based on definite experimentation but rather on what he thought would work.

Serious research began in the 1930s in Alabama and Illinois. At Auburn University, H. S. Swingle and E. V. Smith built small ponds to study experimental management and stocking because Alabama had a paucity of natural lakes,

poor stream fishing, and at the time, few reservoirs. At the Illinois Natural History Survey, David Thompson and George W. Bennett studied fish populations in lakes and ponds. As Bennett wrote in "A Century of Biological Research," "Thompson believed that the food resources and carrying capacity of a body of water remained fairly constant but that the number of fish could vary widely. He reasoned that, if the weight of the fish remained constant, then the removal of some fish would furnish more food per individual for those remaining, and the growth rate would increase; if more fish were planted, less food would be available per individual, and the growth rate would decrease." Other researchers elsewhere, notably R. W. Eschmeyer and W. F. Carbine in Michigan, were doing studies along much the same track. Eschmeyer poisoned the entire populations of several small lakes for which the fishing was poor, and instead of a scarcity of fish he found an "overabundance" of stunted fish. Studying the spawning of centrarchids, Carbine found that many more young were produced than the lake could support. Slowly, the principles of modern fishery management for bass began to evolve, and in time Bennett was able to argue against stocking, closed seasons, and length and creel limits for bass. Bennett's work on largemouth bass in experimental Ridge Lake, which he studied and controlled for more than thirty years, is of the utmost importance to the understanding of the species (it is discussed at length in Chapter 4).

Starting in the 1920s and 1930s, construction of flood-

control reservoirs and huge "multipurpose" impoundments, particularly in the South and West, vastly increased the extent of public fishing water. In 1900 there were only about 100 reservoirs more than 500 acres in size in the U.S. As of 1980 there are 1600 reservoirs totaling more than ten million acres. And this figure does not include "run of the river" lock and dam impoundments, which total more than a million acres. Not counting the Great Lakes and Alaska, reservoirs now account for almost half of all standing public fishing waters in the country. Add to this one million farm ponds, and the suitability of many for bass, plus the increase in leisure time and income since the end of World War II, and one can understand the tremendous burgeoning of interest in bass fishing.

Two men, Elwood (Buck) Perry and Ray Scott, have had a significant impact on modern-day bass fishing. More than thirty years ago Perry embarked on a systematic method of fishing that he called "spoonplugging," because he had devised a lure, a spoonplug, that would crawl across the bottom. Briefly put, Perry had discovered that bass, big bass, spend much of their time deep in "sanctuaries" in a lake. He also observed that bass leave their sanctuaries by certain "migration routes" to feed, and so in order to catch bass it is necessary to discover their sanctuaries, migration routes, and feeding grounds. Bass can be caught in any one of these areas, but the key to big success is locating the sanctuary where the bass are holed up. In a lake or deep reservoir, the most likely spots to probe are sharp dropoffs, the channel of a submerged creek, a lone boulder at the end of a sand bar, flooded timber, old building foundations, stone walls, and even graveyards—in short, anything on the bottom that is different from the surrounding area. Fishermen now call such areas "structure," and "structure fishing" is the name of the game today for bass. Structure is so important to bass that some fishermen have taken to creating their own by toppling trees into a lake. A fallen tree will concentrate bass within a week. Better yet, a fisherman will pull a tree out into a lake behind his boat and anchor it in deep water to create his own private "honey hole."

Knowledgable bass fishermen will also use the term "pattern." "What's the pattern on the bass?" one fisherman will ask another. Pattern is an all-inclusive term that embraces structure, temperature, the depth of the fish, water clarity, the type of cover, the type of lure color, and lure presentation. Anyone interested in keeping up with the latest lingo or developments should read *Bassmaster*, the magazine published by BASS, the acronym for the Bass Anglers Sportsmen Society in Montgomery, Alabama. The boss of BASS is Ray Scott, an Auburn graduate with a silver tongue and a golden touch. As Scott once remarked of his own powers of persuasion, "Boy, can I talk. When I was a kid on the same football team with Bart Starr, he was the center and I was the quarterback!"

For ten years Scott worked as an insurance man, a job that gave him countless ways to practice reaching people. In

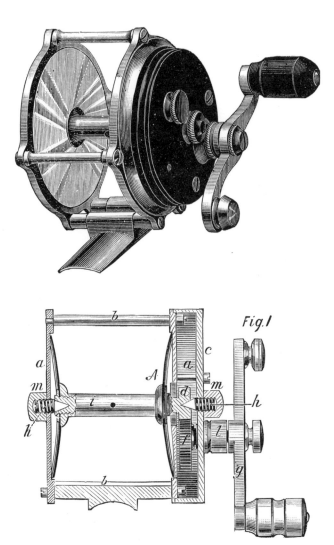

1967, at the age of thirty-four, Scott quit insurance to found BASS. He rented a tiny office and set out to recruit members at annual dues of ten dollars a head. Using the same kind of referral system he had used to find insurance prospects, he began soliciting members in person and through the mail. Always on the alert for any doings regarding bass, I was intrigued by Scott's brochures that came in the mail, and I filed him away in the back of my head with the notion of doing a story on him and BASS in the future for *Sports Illustrated.* The opportunity came in September of 1969 when Scott was staging the All-American Invitational Tournament on Lake Ouachita near Hot Springs, Arkansas. I called Scott to say that I would fly down to cover the tournament for *SI.* He was elated. As I found out when I met him, none of the major outdoor magazines had given BASS notice because they were suspicious of fishing tournaments. BASS then had 7000 members and was growing daily. Today BASS has 350,000 members, and Scott has become a millionaire many times over.

Some of the bass fishermen Scott rustled up starting BASS have become famous in their own right. There is Bill Dance, whom Scott found years ago when he had an hour and a half layover in Memphis. "I got me a pocketful of nickels and started workin' the phone booth," Scott recalls. "I remember the name from the Yellow Pages, Lake View Marina, and I said, 'We're lookin' for some sure-'nuff high-class bass fishermen,' and the manager of the marina said, 'There's a young feller here named Dance, and he's better than any-

one.'" Dance joined BASS. So did fishermen who also became stars on the BASS circuit, such as Roland Martin, the top BASS tournament money winner of all time; Tom Mann, a former Alabama game warden who now manufactures a number of leading lures, including the lead minnow spinner named "Little George" after Governor Wallace; and Johnny Morris of Springfield, Missouri, who is on his way to becoming a tycoon with his authorized "Bass Pro Shops" strewn across the country.

In 1975, with support from BASS, the American Fishing Tackle Manufacturers Association, the National Audubon Society, James Heddon Sons, Pflueger Corporation, and a host of other backers, the Sports Fishing Institute in Washington, D.C., sponsored the First National Bass Symposium. The fifty-seven papers presented at the symposium, published as a book, *Black Bass Biology and Management,* are important, but the true value of the symposium was that it recognized nationally for the first time the great ecological and economic importance that bass have come to occupy in American life.

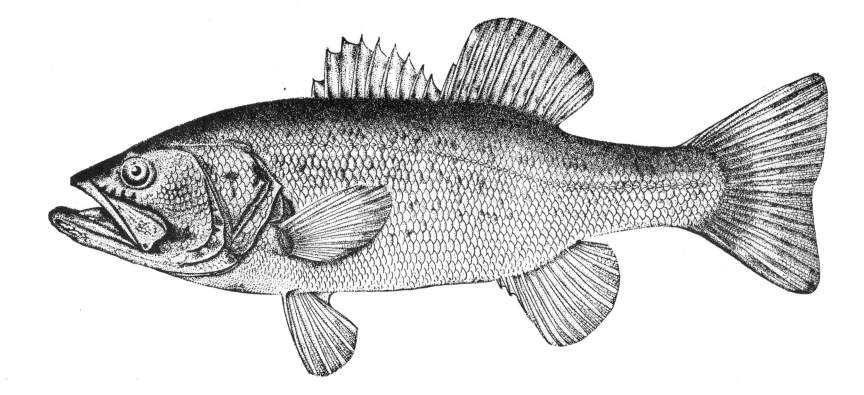

The rugged largemouth bass has at last attained recognition as the leading freshwater gamefish in the United States.

A favorite food of bass, golden shiners school for protection.

half to four pounds of fish.

As a young bass feeds and resumes growth, its scales grow. It retains the same scales throughout life, and the cessation or slowing of growth during the winter leaves a mark on the scales which resembles a ring in the cross section of a tree trunk. A biologist examining a scale through a microscope can count the rings or "annuli" to determine the age of an individual bass. In general, bass in the north can live longer than those in the south. Largemouth bass in northern Wisconsin have been known to reach fifteen years of age, while the longest-lived bass from Louisiana was eleven.

The year-old bass, which can be anywhere from two to eight or even fourteen inches long, depending on the food supply, genetic makeup, and length of growing season, feeds on a variety of prey. Besides insects, it preys on fingerling fishes, including those of its own species. A bass is capable of eating any organism whose maximum width can fit inside its own bucket-like mouth.

Adult bass will also eat frogs, salamanders, and other amphibians, hatchling turtles and small snakes, and even small mammals and birds. Despite this omnivorous diet bass cannot necessarily swallow everything they seize. I once tossed a twelve-inch eel (*Anguilla rostrata*) into an aquarium that contained eight largemouths, the biggest being three and a half pounds. This big one grabbed the eel immediately and swallowed it—or at least tried to. But lo, the eel's tail began to poke through the gill flap. The startled bass relinquished its grip and the eel shot free through the flap. In an instant another bass seized the eel, but the eel again wriggled free through the gill flap. The eel did this to every frenzied bass in the tank. Sometimes the eel poked its head through first, as if for variation. On several occasions the eel would be working its way through the gill flap of one bass only to have another bass grab it. The eel would thread its way through both. Finally the three-and-a-half pound bass hit the eel a second time, and the eel, exhausted from playing Houdini, disappeared down the gullet of the bass for good. In the wild, the eel doubtless would have escaped.

A bass feeds in two ways. It will ingest a soft-bodied creature such as an earthworm simply by cavitation. By suddenly opening its mouth, the bass creates a space into which water rushes, carrying the food. Any earth or debris is then expelled through the gill covers. Bass also grasp and gulp. When a bass seizes a fish as prey, it does not bite or chew. It grasps the prey any way it can with its bristle-like teeth on the upper and lower lips. The bass will then try to swallow the prey head first. If the prey is held from the rear or the side, the bass will turn it around to swallow it head first, so that the dorsal fin of the prey will lie flat when drawn into the mouth and throat. When bass are on a feeding spree, they might stock up on a number of minnows and hold them inside their mouths. I have looked into the mouth of a feeding bass and seen a half dozen minnows lying there like so many people in bed. When the prey enters the throat, it is crushed by the pharyngeal teeth.

Here are a couple of other observations about feeding bass.

Even a duckling makes an attractive meal for a hungry largemouth.

Having watched them feed for years, I can tell when they are in a feeding mood. True, this mood with bass in captivity might have been triggered by an action of mine—bass are very responsive to learning cues and will quickly learn to come to hand for food—but there was no mistaking that they were hungry and wanted to eat. When a bass wants to eat, its eyes usually assume a reddish glow as though they had been plugged into a socket. The eyes just light up. Moreover, the fish erects its spiny dorsal fin, as if to signal battle stations for the attack. A bass will do this when attracted by a fluttering on the surface of the water, as might be caused by a struggling dragonfly or moth. The eyes will glow, the spiny dorsal fin will stand erect, and the fish will then turn and wheel for the attack. If uncertain of the nature of the disturbance, the bass might put on the brakes an inch or two away from the fluttering as if to give it the once-over. The dragonfly may suddenly cease moving, but let there be one twitch, one sign of life, and the bass will seize it without hesitation. (Bass also erect their spiny dorsal fins when agitated, excited, or frightened. The response reminds me of the way a rooster will raise his hackles or a dog his ruff.)

None of the above really answers what the bass fisherman forever has in mind: If the bass had their druthers, what food would they prefer? As a general rule, fish eat what is most readily available, but in an effort to determine what bass preferred if given a choice, William M. Lewis and his colleagues at Southern Illinois University conducted a series of experiments. Lewis tested various combinations of prey,

based on their importance as natural food and as bait, on wild bass held in stock watering tanks. As near as was practical, Lewis fed the bass various prey of the same size. When the results of the tests were added up, they showed that bass having their druthers ate golden shiners more readily than any other food. Indeed, in some instances they fed on the shiners to the exclusion of other available prey, and in the majority of experiments they ate the shiners more than twice as frequently as any other prey. Interestingly, the larger bass had more difficulty in catching shiners than other prey, but the constant movement of the shiners apparently excited the bass into pursuit.

After golden shiners, the preferred foods, in order, were bluegill sunfish, green sunfish, bullheads, and white crappies. Feeding on crayfish was variable, and in some cases the bass did not eat them at all. The bass preferred natural-colored goldfish to gold-colored goldfish. Toads were not eaten when leopard frogs were available. "Another item of interest was the behavior of the bass when food was thrown into the tanks," Lewis reported. "Sometimes a tank contained a particular food item for several days without its being eaten. When a specimen of the same item was thrown into the tank, however, it was usually taken at the instant it hit the water."

During the test, the bass daily consumed an average amount of forage equal to 2.2 percent of its body weight. During a two-week period in the spring the bass ceased feeding or fed sparingly, and the cessation "appeared to be associated with a stage in sexual development."

Largemouth bass feed primarily by sight. They see their prey and then strike. However, there are important differences between the eyes of a bass and those of a human being. First of all, no fish, including the bass, has true eyelids. The bass sleeps with its eyes open. (To us this may appear difficult to do, but think about this: we sleep with our ears open.) Actually, our own eyelids are not so much for covering our eyes when we sleep as they are for keeping the eyes moist and clean while we are awake. Inasmuch as the bass lives in water, it has no need of eyelids because particles of dirt cannot collect on its eyes.

A second important difference is that a bass has its eyes on the sides of its head while ours are in front. A bass thus has a far greater field of vision than we do. It can see in all directions except directly below or directly behind. As Carl L. Hubbs and Reeve M. Bailey pointed out in their study *The Small-Mouthed Bass,* "The increase in the size of the visual field is gained at the expense of binocular vision, which is essential, at least in humans, in accurately judging distances. In looking at any object both of our eyes are focused upon it, and the convergence of the two views thus obtained makes it possible for us to estimate distances rather accurately (the simple experiment of trying to bring two pencil points into contact with one eye closed will make this principle of binocular vision clear). A bass can have binocular vision only in a very limited field directly in front of the head. Since feeding bass directly face their prey, it is likely that they are able to judge the distance necessary for the strike."

Actually, a bass has no great need to have binocular vision over a long range. We live in air where we can see long distances, but the bass lives in water where visibility is limited because particles in the water scatter light. This helps to account for still another difference between the eyes of bass and man. The lens of the human eye is flattened. At rest, human eyes are far-sighted, easily perceiving objects at long distances but not those close up. To see close up we need to move muscles to change the shape of the lenses from flat to spherical. By contrast, the bass at rest is normally near-sighted since the lenses of its eyes are not flat but rigidly spherical. This is as it should be, for the bass is more interested in what lies close at hand than a great way off. At rest, the eyes of a bass take in about a foot on either side. Still, if need be the bass can change focus and switch from being near-sighted to far-sighted, although the maximum distance a bass can see is only thirty to forty feet in very clear water. Even then, the bass would not clearly discern an object but see it as a blur through haze. If the object were a lure, whether or not a hungry bass reacted would undoubtedly depend, as we shall see, on the color and/or flash of the lure and its rate of movement through the water. The bass might also perceive noise or vibrations made by the lure, but these would be detected not by sight but by hearing or what has been called the "sixth sense" of the lateral line, about which more later.

*As seen from below, a largemouth pursues a
fisherman's plug running just below the surface.*

Here is a sequence of photographs showing how
the largemouth bass reacts to an underwater plug.
In the picture below, the fish spots a plug as it
moves overhead. Notice the glow to the eyes.

The fish gives chase.

*A foot or so behind the plug, the bass opens its
mouth to seize it.*

*Suddenly caught by the hooks, the bass twists and
turns to get free.*

Flexing its jaws violently, the bass attempts to eject the plug.

In a final effort, the fish leaps from the water in a desperate attempt to throw the plug.

Bass are put off by bright sunlight, and they most often feed at daybreak and dusk, and at different hours during a day that is overcast. In testing largemouth bass and other fishes at the Shedd Aquarium in Chicago, Gene Ciampi was able to use lights to simulate dawn, dusk, cloudy weather, and bright sunlight. He found that on a cloudy overcast day, all species were most active from dawn to midmorning and from midafternoon to dusk. By contrast, they were the least responsive to lures and natural foods under direct bright sunlight and immediately after dark.

Without question, bass not only see color but discriminate between colors, and some colors evoke more response than others. Briefly put, bass see colors as much as a man would if he looked at them through a yellow filter. The classic experiment of color perception in largemouth bass was conducted by Frank A. Brown, Jr., in 1935 at the Illinois Natural History Survey. Until Brown's work color perception had been a subject of debate, but Brown not only took all debate out of the matter but came up with valuable insights into the ability of bass to learn from experience.

Brown placed young bass one to two inches long in white enamel basins. There was water in the basins and one bass to each basin. Brown then took a number of pipettes or eyedroppers and marked them in different colors. He filled some of the colored eyedroppers with live food, *Daphnia* and mosquito larvae, and he attached electrical wiring to the other eyedroppers. Depending on which color eyedroppers were given to the bass they got either food or a weak shock. Using this system of reward and punishment, Brown found that the bass most readily distinguished red, followed in decreasing order by yellow, white, green, blue, and black. Again, and this is most significant for fisherman, Brown discovered that the bass learned "more quickly to avoid an unpleasant stimulus than to react positively to a pleasant one." As Brian Curtis remarks of this finding in *The Life Story of the Fish*, "In terms of survival value in the wild, this is understandable: one single failure to avoid death (presumably unpleasant) is fatal, whereas failure to approach food (presumably pleasant) may be repeated quite often without bringing the end."

Other studies confirm this. In a laboratory study by Arthur Witt, largemouth bass fingerlings quickly learned to avoid an earthworm on a hook but take those free of the hook. Moreover, the rate of the angling catch on lakes studied in Illinois, Kentucky, and Alabama suddenly declined after opening day, as though the bass readily learned that lures were dangerous.

Without question, the color or colors of a lure are of importance in getting a largemouth to strike. Reporting on the effectiveness of various colors for lures used on largemouth bass in Ridge Lake, Dr. George W. Bennett of the Illinois Natural History Survey wrote in *Management of Lakes and Ponds* that "studies made in the daytime indicated that red and white casting baits had a catch rate for largemouth bass of 3.5 times that of the next most often listed color, which was black. Among fly rod lures, yellow seemed to be the color most acceptable to the largemouths; white or combinations of white and other colors caught the second greatest number of fish. Black lures were important in both casting and fly rod sizes; some fishermen believe that fish strike black lures because they see these baits poorly and strike out of curiosity. Black plugs that create a disturbance at the surface of the water are often very effective for night fishing. Fish swimming below such a surface lure at night follow the water disturbance and may see the indefinite outline of the lure."

For 15 years I kept largemouth bass in captivity in aquaria. The principal aquarium I used was almost six feet long, two feet wide, two feet deep, and contained 120 gallons of water. With proper aeration, I kept as many as twenty-two adult bass in it at one time without ill effect.

Intrigued by the attraction of bass to the color red, I wondered if they would be more likely to hit a red minnow than one of another color. The standard live bait sold where I live is the drab killifish (*Fundulus heteroclitus*) from the Hudson River, and although it is an extremely hardy fish (in laboratory tests it has lived in salt water with three times the salinity of seawater), the killifish is not as effective a live bait as shiners, but these are hard to come by and very delicate.

As the result of various experiments with a number of dyes, I decided that neutral red was far the best dye to use on killies. It was not toxic, at least not in the minute amounts I used, it turned the killies red, and the killies retained the

color for a day or two. I was able to dye a dozen or more killies at one time simply by dropping a couple of pinches of neutral red into a water jug with the fish and swishing it around for a period of time.

For my first test, I had half a dozen acclimated largemouth bass in the big aquarium, when I dumped in twenty-four killies, twelve dyed red and twelve naturally dull. I kept score with a pad and pencil. The bass were after the fish at once and the action was frenzied, so frenzied I couldn't make an absolutely accurate count of what disappeared when. Still, there was no question that the reds generally went first at a ratio of about two reds for every natural. I later repeated the experiment a number of times, and almost every time the bass gobbled up the red killies faster. One day I fed the bass worms to take the edge off their appetite, and a couple of hours later I added fourteen killies, seven dyed red. Within half an hour the bass had taken four red killies and only two naturals. Several hours later, only one red killie was left while four naturals remained. Two hours after this, the count was no red and two naturals. There was no question but that bass could see red killies better than naturals. On one occasion, the largest bass, a two-pounder, had to go at the last red killie in the tank. The killie raced up and down on top of the water four or five times before the bass finally nailed it in a corner with a mighty whoosh that sent water slopping over the sides. The red dye simply stood out too much for the killie's safety. By contrast, drab killies shook off bass in hot pursuit simply by

Largemouths seek cover, or what fishermen call "structure." This bass in Lake George, New York, hangs by an old pier.

A bass in a Florida river seeks cover beneath a fallen tree, a classic hangout, as most fishermen know.

Slowly moving with the river current, a largemouth bass adapts its coloration to the bottom.

blending into the weeds and rocks in the aquarium.

Although bass are primarily sight feeders, other senses play a role. Bass are able to hear, and they can hear in two ways: through their ears, which are buried in the sides of the head, and through the lateral line, a series of pores which runs along each side of the fish from the head to the tail. Precisely where the ears pick up and the lateral line leaves off is not known—both organs are connected to the same part of the nervous system—but as a general rule it can be said that the ears allow bass to hear sounds as we might hear them, while the lateral line allows the fish to detect low-frequency vibrations such as the struggling of an injured minnow. Indeed sound, not sight, may sometimes give a bass the first inkling of prey. Sounds are important to bass, and certain kinds apparently are attractive. If you are underwater and want to attract bass, strike two stones together. Perceptive anglers know that sound can play a part in bringing a lure to the attention of fish, as witness rattle-type lures and popping plugs and bugs, and some fishermen who want to stir up action will slap the water surface with a paddle and then begin casting a few minutes later.

Bass can also smell odors in the water. It is well known that salmon can detect minute odors in water, but how much bass rely on smell is uncertain. Bass have two pairs of nostrils set on each side of the snout as pits. These pits form the anterior and posterior openings of the chambers housing the actual organs of smell, one chamber on each side. As a bass moves its jaws in breathing, it pumps water in and out of the nostrils. The fish is thus able to sample the chemistry of its environment continuously. The general view is that the bass and its sunfish relatives are sight rather than smell oriented, but fishermen who wish to take no chances often put anise on their lures to hide the smell of human odor.

Bass also have a sense of taste, but little is known about it. There are some organisms such as garden slugs and tadpoles (species unknown) that they would take and then expel in aquarium feeding experiments I conducted. Presumably the organisms were distasteful.

Senses and temperature play critical roles in prompting bass to move or migrate within a given body of water. The availability of food also comes into play. Dr. Roy C. Heidinger is of the belief that there is "more movement in a bass population" when threadfin shad and not only gizzard shad are present. Some tagged bass have moved as much as sixteen miles in a year, but as Heidinger writes, "we will never completely understand the movement of bass by observing a single fish. For a complete understanding, we must know what each bass is doing in relation to other bass and forage fishes."

Biologist Mike Lembeck, who tagged Florida largemouths stocked in the San Diego reservoirs with radio transmitters, found the fish holding in very deep water, and in the June 1979 issue of *Outdoor Life*, Jerry Gibbs described the amazing catches made by Ken Locke and other anglers who fish for these bass by trolling leadcore line 100 feet down. In one day Locke landed five Florida largemouths weighing a total of sixty pounds nine ounces, a record for a daily limit in California. The smallest fish weighed ten pounds seven ounces.

Without having lived underwater for at least a year it is perhaps dangerous for me to make any black-and-white statements about the movements of bass, but in ponds it would appear that bass have well-defined territories. That, at least, has been my experience with largemouths in two ponds I studied and fished for ten years. One pond was little more than an acre in size, and there the bass, usually the larger ones of two pounds and up, concentrated in a hole ten feet deep near the dam during the summer and fall months. In the other pond, five acres in size and seven feet at its deepest, bass were usually found near certain shoreline objects that offered cover. I recall in particular one fallen tree which seemed to harbor at least one bass in the two- to three-pound class. If I took a fish there, I felt rather sure of being able to find a comparable fish occupying the same territory within a few days to a week.

In an experiment in the wild, Arthur D. Hasler and Warren J. Wisby of the University of Wisconsin studied the territorial or "homing" instinct in largemouth bass in two lakes. They captured the fish by angling and by net during the summer, clipped the fins to mark each fish, and then released them in midlake. Later that same year, they found that 68 percent of the bass had returned to their original sites. The next summer, Hasler and Wisby checked again, and this time they found 77 percent of the bass in areas where they had been captured the previous year. The biolo-

gists wrote in *Ecology*, "It is not known to what extent these fish move about the lake during the winter, although it is known that they leave their summer areas at the lake edge. It is, of course, quite possible that they do not move very far from their 'home' areas."

Certainly in a confined space such as an aquarium bass have well-defined territories. During the years when I kept a series of largemouths in my 120-gallon aquarium, invariably one bass, usually the biggest, would stake out a claim to two-thirds of the tank. This dominant bass would drive the others to the opposite end of the tank and woe to the subordinate bass that crossed a couple of bricks I had used to mark the dividing line. The dominant bass would rush at the intruder and nip viciously at it. On occasion the dominant bass would keep up the attack even after it had chased the intruder back into its own end of the tank, and there the subordinate would apparently signal surrender by angling its head down sharply toward the bottom and cramping its fins. The dominant bass was always aggressive in defending its territory, even when well fed. Over a period of time, say three to six months, the dominant bass would almost always kill off all the other bass in the tank by harrying them to death.

Among the subordinate bass themselves there appeared to be a pecking order with the fish occupying different stations. It appeared to me that the most dominant bass of the subordinate group would usually occupy the bottom portion of the tank while the others were stacked above. If I re-

This pair of bass, which have just moved in over a grass and sand bottom, are in a solid color phase.

This bass shows still another phase of coloration.
It is light on the bottom and dark on the top.

moved this fish from the tank, the bass that was the next most aggressive in the subordinate group would take over the vacated territory.

Whenever I introduced a new bass that was larger than the dominant bass into the tank, the newcomer would be forced to stay with the subordinate bass, but then after a day or two it would challenge the dominant bass and take over its territory. (I never sexed the bass to determine whether or not the dominant bass was male or female, but I am of the opinion that dominance of the tank depended solely on size.)

When I put other species of fishes in the tank, the largemouth ruled even when smallmouth were of comparable size, perhaps because the smallmouth were almost always "nervous" in the aquarium. With sunfish, white perch, yellow perch, and other species, it was no contest. The largemouth ruled without question. Trout were also cowed, except on one occasion when a plump ten-inch brown trout took over and chased the bass, which were larger, to the smaller end. This was the only time I ever saw a trout exert dominance, but this one ruled the tank, and in the course of five or six months killed off the largemouths after constant attack. After a year of watching this trout dominate the tank against all comers, I returned it alive and well to the Croton River.

Above and beyond such questions of dominance, territory, migration, senses, spawning, and food preference, one question remains dominant in the mind of a bass fisherman: What can I do to make them hit?

In an attempt to answer that question, my colleague Gene Ciampi, who was a psychologist before becoming a professional photographer, spent considerable time at the John G. Shedd Aquarium in Chicago testing largemouth bass and other fish for *Sports Illustrated*. As a result, he was able to rank fish species on "intelligence," defined here as wariness in striking a lure; moreover, he was also able to discover why different species are attracted to different lures or movement of the lure even when they were gorged with food.

Ciampi's tests at the Shedd Aquarium were conducted under just about ideal experimental conditions. Inasmuch as he had the cooperation of aquarium authorities, he was able to control both lighting and feeding conditions to test the fish in aquatic environments that closely simulated their natural habitat. He had no disturbances from the public in the course of doing his research. As a matter of fact, the habitat was the equivalent of virgin wilderness waters in a way, even though he and the fishes were in the middle of Chicago, because no one had worked them over with a plug or a spoon or flies. They were, in short, absolute rookies when it came to lures.

Despite this, some of the species, especially the largemouth and smallmouth bass, were at once very suspicious of any artificial lure cast to them. By contrast, some other species, notably the brook trout, were remarkably slow in learning the difference between real food and imitations. In between tests Ciampi let the fishes go without food for sev-

Another favorite place for bass is near or under a weedbed.

eral days, but even then the reactions to the various lures stayed the same for the different species of fishes, and all the time the largemouth bass was the most reluctant of any to go after artificial lures.

Ciampi was convinced that the largemouth bass had a brain superior to those of the other species he tested at the Shedd Aquarium. After repeated tests, the largemouth showed the highest levels of discernment. The smallmouth was close behind, and as a matter of fact both species of black bass had many behavioral characteristics or traits in common. Along with muskies, the largemouth and small-mouth bass not only demonstrated the most suspicion but they were the only three species out of the eight tested that would not take an artificial lure after any other fish in the tank had struck it. Pending further research, Ciampi's guess was that these species have a communication system of some sort which actually enables them to warn each other of danger.

In the other five species this ability to communicate, if that is what it is, either did not exist or was not sufficiently developed to be of use. Certainly Ciampi found no indication of it with trout, bluegills, or crappies.

To be sure, Ciampi was able to get largemouth and small-mouth bass to strike a lure in his tests, but this would happen only once. After that, they refused to strike the lure tested, and he had to let the fish rest several days before trying a new lure on them. The same was true with muskies and northern pike. Possibly this may explain the sudden success of a new lure in bass waters. It is successful because the bass do not recognize it as a lure.

In contrast to the bass, several species would not only strike at anything cast their way, ranging from a bottle cap to a spoon, but would often hit the same lure a second or third time. Again the brook trout fell into this category. It took a bass only one experience to learn that a lure was not food, but the brook trout had to have this drummed into its head two or three times.

As Ciampi tested the fish he scored their responses, and when the tests were concluded he ranked the different species for "intelligence." The largemouth was number one. The smallmouth was number two. The muskie ranked third and the northern pike fourth. The brook trout was fifth, the bluegill sunfish sixth, the crappie seventh, and the gar eighth and last.

None of this means that the bass fisherman should give up seeking his game because they are too smart. Far from it. It became obvious to Ciampi that no matter how "smart" or "dumb" the various species were, certain lures definitely had more appeal than others.

The effectiveness of a lure depended on three factors: the color, the action, and the sound it made in the water. As a general rule, all the species tested showed a preference for lures that closely resembled natural food. But similarity of the color to the natural food was more important in getting a fish to strike than similarity of shape to the natural food. Ciampi observed this while testing muskies. The keepers at

Pickerel, such as the one in the foreground, often occupy the same waters as the largemouth in the East.

A chain pickerel can compete with bass for food—or a plug. This fish is going after a plug cast by a bass fisherman.

Unlike the largemouth, the pickerel prefers to lie in ambush for its prey. In this sequence of photographs, the pickerel displays its method of attack. Below, a pickerel is motionless in the grass. But wait...

The pickerel sees a sunfish, and it suddenly shoots forward like a torpedo.

With a lightning-like strike, the pickerel instantly seizes the sunfish and hurries away with its prey, leaving behind a cloud of silt stirred up by the explosive encounter.

*In order not to lose its catch to other predators the
pickerel heads for the weeds, looking for all the
world like the fox that raided the henhouse.*

the Shedd Aquarium regularly fed the muskies goldfish, and when he tested the muskies they responded best to bright-gold lures, even when the shape and size of the lures were not similar to a real-life goldfish. Although less discriminating feeders such as the brook trout and crappies would often strike at anything, they did show the greatest response to light-colored shiny lures, such as a small spinner. For all fish, the least effective colors were black and dark red. Lures these colors did not reflect or pick up light, particularly in murky water.

Ciampi found that he could not drag a lure back through the water and expect to catch fish—fish were not interested. But when Ciampi altered the retrieve with sharp sporadic jerks, the fish perked up, and they really became interested when the sharp sporadic jerks were combined with a regular side-to-side action or flutter.

Sound was enticing in a lure. If a lure had sound, it usually was an added plus, and this was particularly true for large-mouth and smallmouth bass. One of the reasons a bright, noisy lure with action attracted attention was because it was utterly foreign to the fish's environment. When a popping bug created an unusual disturbance, fish apparently regarded it not just as a meal but as an annoyance or a threat. This would provoke a fish into striking, even when it was not interested in food. Largemouth and smallmouth bass were the hardest to trick into mistaking a lure for food, but they were the easiest to annoy into striking when a lure entered their territory.

Ciampi also discovered that even during the times of maximum activity, all the fish underwent dormant periods in which they neither moved nor fed. These dormant periods or rest periods would last from two minutes to two hours. Whatever the duration, the dormant periods came and went with no definable pattern. One moment a bass or a pike might be feeding or on the prowl, and in the next minute its fins would barely move and it would hang near the bottom as though asleep. Not all the fish rested or became dormant at the same time during the day. A largemouth bass might suddenly decide to rest while the other fish in the tank moved about. The moving fish merely ignored the fish that was resting. When fish were dormant they usually would not strike. Ciampi was fascinated to watch a dormant muskie. When a muskie was on the feed, a goldfish thrown into the tank barely had time to move a fin before it was struck. When dormant, however, this same muskie would appear almost oblivious to a goldfish.

The return to periods of activity came suddenly. There was no prolonged wake-up period. Almost as though a bell had rung, activity abruptly resumed, and a lure which seconds before had no appeal might very well be pursued and hit.

As a result of both testing fishes at the Shedd Aquarium and his own considerable time spent underwater in the wild observing largemouth bass, Ciampi has five tips to offer fishermen:

1. Don't believe that a pond or a lake has necessarily been "fished out." I have been underwater in lakes and ponds so described, and I have seen bass in them. The fact is the bass have learned to be wary of fishermen and their lures, and the only way to take them is to try the unconventional.

2. Never rely on the built-in action of a lure to catch bass. The more movement a fisherman gives to a lure by jerking, twitching or bobbing it, the more appealing it will be to the fish.

3. If not successful, use lures that are different from those ordinarily used. If you don't have anything unusual in your tackle box, alter the color or the action, no matter how wild or offbeat the new offering may look.

4. Although it has been said that God does not deduct fishing time from an angler's allotted span, and while it also has been said that you should fish whenever you get the chance, try to avoid the middle of the day with its direct bright sunlight when fish are relatively inactive. And on overcast days particularly, make sure the lure you use is bright enough to be visible and noisy enough to be heard.

5. If a bass does not strike on the first three casts, change the lure. After three lures, try a different fishing spot. Nine times out of 10, an unproductive cast means the bass are not there or that if they are, they are wise to the fisherman. When they are wise, only a wiser fisherman will catch them.

Bass do not live forever. By the time a year class has reached its fourth year, the great majority of them have perished. Among bass predators are other fishes (notably gar, pike, and muskies), reptiles (watersnakes, snapping turtles, and alligators), various birds (such as kingfishers, mergansers, herons, pelicans, loons, ospreys, and eagles), minks, otters (as shown on page 000), and, of course, man. Bass and other fishes can also be killed by suffocation in the so-called winter or summer kills. Winter kills, which are more common, occur when snow blankets the ice of a pond or lake and prevents photosynthesis. Then the oxygen may be depleted by the respiration of plants and animals and the demands of organic decay. Parasites and diseases may also play a role. Although parasites and diseases may not necessarily cause death (they don't in the majority of instances), they nevertheless can debilitate fish so they become vulnerable to predators. An example is the parasitic yellow grub (*Clinostomum marginatum*), sometimes found in the muscles of bass. This parasite matures in the great blue heron, with snails serving as the intermediate host. Fish heavily infected with yellow grub swim more slowly and are thus more readily caught by predators. Still another parasite of concern is the bass tapeworm (*Protocephalus ambloptilis*), which may cause sterility in the female fish and for which no cure is known.

Above and beyond such concerns is the toll that pollution may have. Water pollution is a national disgrace in the United States, affecting not only bass and other natural resources but the very lives of people. Within the last ten years

A muskie grabs a goldfish thrown to it by photographer and psychologist Ciampi, who tested eight different species of fish for their "intelligence." He found that largemouth bass were the "smartest" in that they were the hardest to fool with a lure.

A muskie lunges for a plug. Although muskies showed a preference for live food, Ciampi discovered that they could be induced to strike a lure because of its movement. "It will not strike a second time the same morning," Ciampi says, "but that first strike often seemed so overpowering that the fish was unable to control it."

The muskie takes the plug. Ciampi was fascinated to observe that this voracious fish often had dormant periods when it would pay no attention to a plug, no matter how much or how often the plug was jiggled in front of its nose.

Out of its dormant period, this muskie is hooked on a spoon. The species ranked third after largemouth and smallmouth bass in "intelligence" in Ciampi's tests.

Attracted by a spinner, a schooling crappie gets set
to strike. Crappies ranked next to last in
"intelligence," which may help to explain why
fishermen often catch one crappie after another.

A bluegill sunfish takes a wet fly while a brook trout falls sucker for a spoon. Unlike a wily largemouth or smallmouth, the brook trout would often hit a lure again and again before realizing it was not food.

there has been a great effort to clean up rivers, streams, and lakes, but the abatement effort, commendable as it might seem, focused on disease-causing organisms in sewage and the oxygen-consuming wastes from industries. The effort was aimed at preventing infectious waterborne diseases and at allowing fish and other aquatic life to thrive. But, scandalously, these new treatment plants have been unable to remove the hundreds of insidious compounds that have come from the growth of the chemical and petrochemical industries since World War II. As a result, many of the major rivers and lakes in the U.S. are laced with such synthetic organic chemicals as carbon tetrachloride, polychlorinated biphenyls (PCBs), and literally hundreds of others. These poisons have been let free to disrupt aquatic food webs, accumulate in fish and other wildlife, or as Dr. Robert Harris of the Environmental Defense Fund has put it, "end up as a chemical alphabet soup in a glass of drinking water or the morning cup of coffee of citizens who mistakenly believed their drinking water had been purified." So far, almost 700 chemicals have been found in drinking water across the U.S., and a number of them are capable of causing cancer, among other harmful effects.

The most widespread are PCBs, which have caused cancer in rats and mice. Widely used by industry because of their heat resistance, PCBs are almost literally everywhere in the country. The Food and Drug Administration has imposed a "temporary tolerance" level of five parts per million (ppm) of PCBs in fish in interstate commerce—a level that a number of scientists believe too high to be safe—but in some bodies of water the levels run far higher than that in fish which can bioaccumulate PCBs to a horrendous degree. A largemouth bass taken from the Hudson River, where the General Electric Company dumped in PCBs for years, had 53.81 ppm of PCBs. What effect PCBs have on bass themselves is not known, but the U.S. Fish and Wildlife service regards 0.5 ppm of PCBs in any fish egg as a source of biological trouble. This is small comfort, especially when one realizes that the U.S. Environmental Protection Agency calculates that ten million pounds of PCBs contaminate the environment each year through vaporization, leaks, and spills.

For all this, the federal and state governments are doing next to nothing to deal with the problem of chemical contamination. The likelihood is that the mess is going to get worse before it gets better, and it won't ever get better until the bass fishermen and trout fishermen and anyone else who cares about natural resources and human health raise absolute hell.

The largemouth does not live alone in its environment, and other fish species, notably the bluegill sunfish, can depress the bass population by sheer force of numbers.

4/
The
Ecology
of Bass

The late George Bennett, who died in 1977, was an original thinker on largemouth bass and warm-water fishery management, and his work is basic to any understanding of largemouth bass ecology. There may be those scientists or fishermen who disagree with his findings, or at least his interpretations of them, but as he himself remarked in his last major paper "Ecology and Management of Largemouth Bass," "It is tremendously difficult to get people to discard old theories when it comes to fishing, and it is easy to disregard known points of fish ecology when they don't coincide with a fisherman's own theories."

Born in Nebraska, Bennett received his Ph.D. at the University of Wisconsin where Aldo Leopold was one of his professors, and Leopold's concepts of the ecological principles of game management were to have a strong influence on Bennett's fishery investigations. In 1938 Bennett joined the Illinois Natural History Survey and in 1943 was appointed head of the Aquatic Biology Section. He later also served as professor of zoology at the University of Illinois. The author or co-author of a number of scientific papers, Bennett also wrote *Management of Lakes and Ponds*, which appeared in a second edition in 1971, and as Ray Scott of BASS once said of the book, "There's wisdom on every page." As a man, scientist, and administrator, Bennett was efficient, kindly, humorous, and generous.

No laboratory-bound technician, Bennett conducted numerous studies in the field, most notably at Ridge Lake in Fox Ridge State Park in central Illinois. Completed in 1941 by the erection of a dam across Dry Run Creek, this eighteen-acre lake was specifically set aside as a study site for largemouth bass under his supervision. For more than thirty years he and survey staff members studied the fish life in the lake and collected data and information on such phenomena as rainfall, thermal stratification, aquatic plants, plankton, bottom fauna, and water transparency. Inasmuch as the dam permitted the lake to be drawn down and all its fish life exposed for census, it has been literally explored from top to bottom. Ridge Lake is a bass biologist's dream, or as Bennett put it with his enthusiasm, "a great toy."

In the spring of 1941 Bennett stocked the new lake with 335 yearling and 100 adult largemouth bass. All the largemouth that have come out of the lake since then, some 35,400 weighing 10,200 pounds as of 1972, are descendants of the original stock of 435 fish.

Starting in 1942 Ridge Lake was opened to public fishing on a highly controlled basis. Fishing was allowed only in June, July, and August when a member of the survey was present. All fishermen had to reserve boats, for which there was no charge, at the laboratory pier. There could be no more than one boat holding a maximum of three fishermen for every two acres of lake. There were no length or creel limits. Fishermen were told to keep all fish caught, no matter how small. When a fisherman returned from fishing, a biologist noted on a special yellow card made out in the fisherman's name the number of hours fished, the number and kinds of fish caught, the length of the fish (to the nearest tenth of an inch), the weight (to the hundredth of a pound), and the baits, live or artificial, used. No restriction was placed on live baits with the exception that no carp, goldfish, or other undesirable species could be used. The biologist also noted any fish with fins clipped during periodic census by the survey, and he also took fifteen to twenty scales from each bass to study age and growth.

One of Bennett's first projects at Ridge Lake was to study the factors that controlled the size and poundage of a population of largemouth bass. At the time, as the result of pond research done in Alabama by H. S. Swingle and E. V. Smith, most fishery biologists believed that the largemouth population depended on the number of other fishes, particularly the bluegill sunfish, on which they could prey for sustenance. The U.S. Soil Conservation Service uncritically adopted the idea and one official, Frank C. Edminster, chief of the Northeast Regional Biology Division of the Soil Conservation Service, optimistically wrote in *Fish Ponds for the Farm*, "The largemouth bass and bluegill sunfish are the best combination to use. They have proved successful and dependable in ponds over much of the country. No other fish have produced as good results."

But as Bennett, who thought highly of the work done in Alabama, was to write in *Management of Lakes and Ponds*, "It soon became evident that the same kinds of fishes that produced satisfactory hook-and-line yields in Alabama ponds, when stocked in the recommended numbers in ponds in other parts of the country, did not behave as they did in Alabama. This was not only because the habitats and fish food complexes were different, but also because the behavior and physiology of the fishes varied within the limits of their natural range. It followed that the program of stocking fingerling bass and bluegills in certain ratios in one part of the country might not produce satisfactory populations for fishing in other regions in spite of the fact that the fish were considered the same."

Nowhere was this made more evident than in Ridge Lake. Up until 1943 Ridge Lake contained only largemouth bass. In the fall of that year Bennett drained the lake and counted each fish. The drainage census revealed that each acre of the lake averaged 48.2 pounds of bass, which made for good fishing and was about what the lake should have produced given its moderately fertile water. Bennett kept the bass alive and returned them to the lake as it refilled. In 1944 he also added 129 bluegill sunfish to see what would happen. In 1945 he drained the lake again, and this time the census revealed that the bass poundage had dropped to 39.6 pound per acre while the bluegills averaged 8.4 pounds per acre. Bennett returned both the bass and the bluegills to the lake, and in 1947 he drained it yet again. This time the bass poundage had dropped further, to 31.5 pounds per acre, while the bluegill poundage had soared to a startling 193.3 pounds per acre. Indeed there were 67,700 individual bluegills descended from the 129 stocked only three years earlier. In sum, the bluegills were by sheer force of numbers depressing the bass population.

The big question was why. Bennett explained that there were several reasons. Largemouth bass are not solely piscivorous (fish-eating) but omnivorous in their diet. Only half their diet is composed of fish. Instead of getting gobbled up by the bass, the prolific bluegills were able to increase rapidly in numbers. By doing this they raised havoc with the bass population by eating the bass fry coming off the nests and also by competing with them for such food as *Daphnia*, *Bosminia*, and other crustacea, insect larvae, and frogs. "As the bluegills go up, the bass go down," Bennett said.

Because of the very way Ridge Lake could be drawn down, Bennett found he was able to control the bluegill population by quickly drawing the water level down fifteen feet in the fall. As the water receded, the bass headed for the bottom and the numerous small bluegills sought cover toward shore where they eventually became stranded. "When there are no predators, man must take their place," Bennett said.

Bennett believed that a number of the findings at Ridge Lake could be applied to the management of reservoir fisheries. "One may say that 'under no circumstances can a large reservoir be biologically compared to the average pond environment!'" he noted in "Ecology and Management of Largemouth Bass," delivered several years before he died. "But we are not comparing physical habitats—we are comparing the behavior of a single species of fish that must hold the same relationship to the other fishes in an aquatic habitat whether in a pond or reservoir. Basic behavior patterns, in my opinion, are similar, regardless of the water." As a

specific case in point, Bennett noted that "Abnormally large bass populations often appear in new reservoirs the first year of impoundment. When a reservoir is first stocked with a variety of adult fishes, factors which limit the success of bass reproduction are largely absent and the bass produce a very large and successful year class, so large, in fact, that the young bass may grow to seven or nine inches and then virtually stop growing (because they run out of food) [or] until thinned by natural mortality (starvation and disease) to some reasonable number. Enough will survive, however, to control reproduction success of all bass for the next three or four spawning seasons. During the same period, numbers of the companion fishes will build up to a point where they begin to make inroads on bass fry, the only point where largemouth bass are highly vulnerable to predation from other members of the sunfish family. The end result is that the bass spawners are never able to produce a new year class of sufficient numerical size to maintain a population in the 10 to 25% (by weight) range."

Bennett observed that anyone seeking to manage a reservoir for bass fishing had to solve this problem of producing new year classes of largemouths, and in his opinion the problem was the same "whether one is dealing with a 16 acre lake or a 25,000 acre reservoir."

The answer to the problem was fluctuating water levels. Bennett cited the lesson of the Illinois River before the flood plains were cut off by man-made levees. Every spring the Illinois would flood thousands of acres of its wide, flat val-ley. Bass and other fishes would invade the new shallows to spawn. Then as the river receded, the numbers of young fish were reduced by predation and stranding. Largemouth bass flourished in this environment. It was nothing to catch a hundred a day.

Bennett also cited the work of R.W. Eschmeyer, who had found that TVA reservoirs with fluctuating water levels had larger populations of game fish than those with stable levels. And then there was his own experience with the drawdowns at Ridge Lake. In brief, the key to production of successful year classes of bass in a reservoir was to lower the water level in the early fall so as to reduce the numbers of rough fish, crappies, and sunfishes. The lake should then be refilled over the winter. "With a lake containing most of the larger fishes of all species but relatively few of the smaller ones, the bass will be able to produce a successful new year class," Bennett observed in "Ecology and Management of Largemouth Bass." "A drawdown done every other year or once in three years should allow the bass to maintain their numbers."

As a result of Bennett's work on Ridge Lake, the state of Illinois did away with a closed season for largemouth bass. "I think the closed season is the silliest law ever concocted," Bennett once told me when I interviewed him for *Sports Illustrated*. "We presume that by closing the season we're going to have a lot of bass, and that isn't true at all. The whole thing revolves around the fact that it isn't the fishermen who control the number of bass, but other fish populations. We know from our experience at Ridge Lake that any time the bluegill population rises above 2000 fish per acre, they're going to start depressing the bass. It's a mistake to close the season, impose a creel limit and a minimum length, and wait for the bass to build up to a big population. The bass never do on this basis.

"There's only one reason for a creel limit on bass that I can think of," he continued, "and that is because some fishermen are successful and others are not. Our studies show that 10 percent of the fishermen—and it's consistently the same 10 percent—catch 80 percent of the bass, and the remaining 90 percent catch only 20 percent. A creel limit stops those 10 percent from making hogs of themselves. There wouldn't be any danger to the fish, but it would be a waste of fish.

"Legal length? What's the basis for legal length? So the bass can reach maturity and spawn? But what difference does it make if one pair of bass is capable of repopulating a lake like this with its own spawn? We know that Ridge Lake won't support more than 2000 bass of assorted sizes, from four inches to nine pounds. Now suppose that in some way you could take 1900 of those bass out of here and leave only 100. And we'll assume that half of those 100 are females. Well, we know from counting eggs and checking broods of young that one of those big females is capable of producing 10,000 young. We know that this lake won't support more than 2000 bass, and yet this one bass can produce five times that. Why impose a length limit so that each bass can reach

sexual maturity? Nobody's going to catch near that many. In our most successful seasons here, fishermen have been able to catch only 60 percent of the available bass, about 50 percent of the total poundage. And that 50 percent—and we think probably more—can be replaced in one season. When bass are taken out, they leave available the food they would have eaten, so the bass that are not caught are capable of growing much more rapidly.

"Fish have indeterminate growth. When you buy a pup, you can say that within a year he will reach mature size, and after that he won't get any larger in bone structure, whether you feed him well or poorly. But a fish keeps growing throughout its life, depending on the amount of food it can swallow and digest. It doesn't grow an inch this year and an inch next year. A fingerling bass in this part of the country can, with good food, get up to eleven inches in one summer. If it has poor feeding, it may be only two and a half inches long at the end of the summer. We've seen bass nine years old and only nine inches long. The only thing that grows are the eyes. Why the eyes grow, I don't know. They're oversized in a stunted fish.

"The danger in the average lake or pond is too many fish rather than too few. The idea is sometimes hard to sell to fishermen. But the fact is, overpopulated ponds often seem to contain no fish. The exceptional fishing found in a naturally primitive environment—before man comes in, settles down, and spoils it—is the result of predation and growth. Predators prevent any one species of fish from becoming

A hungry otter spots a bass. The next four photographs tell the story of the predatory bass turned prey.

*The otter barrels through the water after the
startled bass.*

*Twisting and turning, the otter more than matches
every move the desperate bass makes.*

The chase is over as the undulating otter seizes the bass by the tail, then cradles the fish in its paws and bites the back. Now the otter will take the bass ashore, toy with the flopping fish as a cat will with a mouse, and then finally eat it tail first.

overabundant, because they're continually being thinned out. Those that survive grow rapidly.

"In evolution, fishes represent a very old group. They've been around millions of years. As they evolved, predators came along and evolved with them. As new forms of predators evolved, such as fish-eating birds, reptiles, amphibians, and mammals, the fish evolved to compensate for this, probably by laying more eggs. So over the years, relatively high predation and relatively high production of young became the norm. The welfare of the fish population actually depends on this high predation. If there were not this high predation in primitive areas, the fish would overpopulate the natural environment.

"Here is a good example. When I was out at McCook, Nebraska, we used to take trips to the primitive northern part of the state to fish and hunt. We located a lake five miles long and about a mile wide that was filled with thousands of bullheads. They were whoppers, for bullheads. Most of them went to a pound, a pound and a half. We'd go in with hip boots and use worms, and the limiting factor as to how fast you could catch them was how fast you could put a worm on. They were all big. You'd catch so many that you'd get to the point where you could hardly drag your stringer out of the lake. Now bullheads are notorious for overpopulating and stunting. So it was very unusual to have such consistently large ones.

"One year we got the idea of going duck hunting up there. So we drove all night and arrived just before daybreak. We really thought we were going to have some good shooting, but we never used a shell. We saw no ducks, only the fish-eating, fish-tasting American mergansers. They're tough. You can't eat them. So we had to move to another lake to get mallards. Now a rancher there told us those mergansers came through that bullhead lake, spring and fall, regularly. They'd stay a couple of weeks, and obviously they were culling the small bullheads, thus leaving the big ones for us to catch. The only place where fish-eating birds do damage is in hatcheries or in trout streams where there are concentrations of hatchery-reared trout that have been stocked. And, of course, both of these are artificial situations."

As another example of the benefits of predation, Bennett cited the case history of Reelfoot Lake, a 14,500-acre lake in Tennessee, containing substantial numbers of largemouth bass, sunfish, crappies, and catfish. In the 1930s, commercial fishermen and great numbers of fish-eating birds worked over the lake, all taking the same kinds of fishes as anglers did. On average, anglers caught 0.89 pounds of fish per hour, a very high figure. The largemouth bass *averaged* almost two pounds apiece. In 1936, the total angling catch was 22,124 pounds, while commercial fishermen accounted for almost 625,000 pounds of fish. Fish-eating birds—4000 egrets, 1500 cormorants, 500 Ward's herons, and seven other species— took more than 400,000 pounds of fish. In 1937, the birds, commercial fishermen, and anglers took a total of slightly more than one million pounds of fish from the lake, an average of seventy-two pounds an acre, and the fishing was

A bass cautiously inspects a minnow on a hook before taking it. In a study at Ridge Lake in Illinois, George Bennett found that fishermen were more successful with lures than with live minnows.

considered excellent by all.

Enter the serpent into Eden. Responding to complaints by anglers, the state of Tennessee began placing restrictions on commercial fishing, and in 1955 commercial fishing was finally eliminated. Bass, bluegills, white crappies, and channel catfish began to decline in size. Over the years, the numbers of birds doubtless decreased while the ranks of anglers increased a hundredfold. But in 1953, the anglers caught only about twenty-one pounds of fish per acre. "From the standpoint of the angler, the relationship in 1937 between anglers, commercial fishermen, and fish-eating birds was nearly ideal," Bennett wrote in *Management of Lakes and Ponds*, "as the combined action of these cropping agencies was taking a reasonable annual fish crop. Thus the benefits of an expanding population were evident: fish had food and space to grow."

Studies at Ridge Lake also revealed some interesting findings about fishermen and fishing. Data collected over a seven-year period showed that artificial lures were more effective than live or other natural baits. Plugs, spoons, and spinners fished on eight or more fishing trips caught 768 bass ten inches or longer in 2188 man-hours, a rate of 2.85 man-hours per fish. More bass were caught on underwater plugs than floating plugs, especially when the surface water warmed after June. Fly rod lures took 672 bass ten inches or more in 2150 man-hours, a rate of 3.20 man-hours per fish. Live and other natural baits took 830 bass ten inches or more in 6252 hours of fishing, a rate of 7.53 man-hours per fish.

Minnows and crayfish were by far the most effective live baits. Minnows had an average catch rate of one bass at least ten inches or longer for every four man-hours of fishing, while crayfish took a desirable bass for every 5.3 man-hours.

During one year the average catch rate of bass for all fishermen was one pound in 7.1 hours. Skill helped reduce that rate considerably. One angler had a catch rate of one pound of bass for every 1.76 hours, while another angler had a catch rate of only one pound for every 11.1 hours. "Both were experienced enthusiastic bass fishermen, both used artificial baits and knew the lake well," Bennett wrote in "Largemouth Bass in Ridge Lake, Coles County, Illinois," "yet one man was more than six times as efficient as the other in catching fish."

Studies at Ridge Lake showed a rapid decline in the catch rate following the morning of the first day of fishing and continuing through the next several days until it leveled off. To Bennett, this suggested that bass in the lake quickly became educated to the more common methods anglers used to present artificial baits, and he added, "Observations on the fishing techniques employed by the most successful bass fishermen suggest these men vary techniques much more than do those fishermen who are less successful."

In 1962 fishermen complained that Ridge Lake contained no large bass, but when Bennett drained the lake the next spring, he found that it contained ninety bass that weighed from three and a half to nine pounds. Of these, eleven fish, which were from eight to ten years old, averaged more than six pounds each. It was Bennett's belief that when angling pressure reached more than sixty man-hours a year per acre, the bass became educated, and as another case in point he cited Onized Lake which he studied early in his career. Two acres in size, Onized was small enough to allow an experienced bait caster to cover all the water within an hour or two. In 1939, sixty-two legal-sized bass were taken, twenty-nine in 1940, and only eight early in 1941. Fishermen complained that the lake was fished out. Bennett investigated and found 275 bass, 45 of them legal size, with 12 weighing from three to six pounds.

Florida gar feed mainly on fish, and in waters where they are numerous, they can adversely affect the largemouth population by predation and competition for food.

A channel catfish sweeps along the bottom. This species eats fish, crustaceans, and insects.

A smallmouth bass ingests a bucktail jig. A jig is a good lure to use on smallmouths because it can be made to simulate a crayfish, one of the smallmouth's favorite foods.

5/ The Smallmouth Bass

Smallmouth bass bring to mind northern lakes with rocky ledges and dropoffs, and clear cool streams studded with rocks and boulders. Because of its spectacular leaps, many fishermen deem the smallmouth a better fighter than the largemouth, but for all its feisty reputation the smallmouth is not as "successful" a species as its cousin. Its habitat is more restricted—it does best in lakes at least one hundred acres in size and more than thirty feet deep—and its feeding habits are generally more specialized. Moreover, as a general rule the smallmouth does not grow to match the size of the largemouth even when the two species occupy the same body of water. At this writing, the world-record smallmouth is an eleven-pound fifteen-ounce fish caught by David Hayes of Grayson County, Kentucky, on July 11, 1955, in Dale Hollow Reservoir. Hayes took the fish, which was twenty-seven inches long and thirteen years old, trolling a white Bomber.

It is not unlikely that the smallmouth that breaks that record will also come from Dale Hollow. Billy Westmorland of Celina, Tennessee, who is probably the best known smallmouth specialist in the country, regularly fishes there. An advocate of light tackle (four- to six-pound test line), Westmorland has taken approximately a hundred smallmouth bass weighing more than eight pounds, three more than nine pounds, and one that went ten pounds two ounces. On Christmas Day in 1970, Westmorland almost had the record when a smallmouth that he estimated at fourteen pounds shook the hook after being up to the boat three times. Westmorland's favorite lure is a one-eighth-ounce jig he makes

This feisty smallmouth was all set to attack the hand of photographer Ciampi when he took this unusual picture. Some fishermen rate the smallmouth a better fighter than the largemouth.

and calls the Hoss Fly.

Although the smallmouth prefers cooler water than the largemouth, curiously enough it begins to cease activity when the water temperature drops to 50 degrees Fahrenheit in the fall months. Unlike largemouths, smallmouths become dormant during the winter. Smallmouths are most active in water temperatures ranging from 65 to 71 degrees.

Smallmouth bass spawn in the spring when the temperature nears 60 degrees. In the southern part of its range, the smallmouth will usually begin spawning in April, while in the northern part of its range spawning takes place as late as July. A study of smallmouth populations in Lake Ontario and the Thousand Islands region of the St. Lawrence revealed considerable variation in spawning time within that relatively limited area. Smallmouth in shallow bays began spawning in the latter part of May or early June, while those influenced by the colder waters of Lake Ontario did not spawn until the latter part of June or July.

Like the largemouth, the male smallmouth constructs the nest. Smallmouths prefer to nest near a rock, log, or another submerged object on a bottom composed of gravel, coarse sand, rock, or rubble. Nests have been found at depths ranging from only ten inches to more then twelve feet. Sunlight may play a role in determining the depth of the nest site because deeper nests are made in water of exceptional clarity.

The male guards the fertilized eggs which, depending on temperature, can take from two to ten days to hatch. At 77 degrees Fahrenheit eggs hatch in two days, at 54 degrees in ten days. The number of eggs in a nest can vary from 1000 to almost 10,000. After hatching, the fry feed on their yolk sacs for several days, and then they begin to swim. The swimming fry are black and do not assume the markings of the adult for a period of perhaps weeks. It has been suggested that the blackness of the fry helps protect them from predation because they are similar in size and coloration to frog and toad tadpoles which appear at about the same time. "These tadpoles are not considered very desirable as food, and for this reason they are at least partly immune from attack," George Bennett observed. "Field observations indicate that smallmouth fry are protected to a certain extent during the very early free swimming stages by these similarities to tadpoles."

As is the case with the largemouth, the size of a year class of smallmouth bass is not related to the number of spawning adults. Sudden changes in temperature during the egg and fry stages appear to play a key role in determining the size of the year class. Temperature also plays a role in the growth of smallmouth because growth is seasonal. In the 1960s Daniel W. Coble analyzed the relationship between mean surface water temperatures for several different smallmouth bass populations in the U.S. and Canada for the months of July through September. He found that the warmer the water, the more the bass from three to five years of age grew.

Albert L. Tester, who studied the food of smallmouths in

Ontario waters, found that food taken by both the fry and adults was conditioned by (1) the size of the food in relation to the size of the bass, and (2) by the relative abundance of food of suitable size in a given habitat. As the fry grow, they eat copepods, cladocerans, small chironomid larvae and pupae, and then larger insects. When about five centimeters long, the fish eat other fish, insects, and crayfish, a diet that is similar to that of the adults. Crayfish are a major part of the diet. Tester reported that in Georgian Bay and Lake Nipissing crayfish accounted for 79 percent of the diet of the adult smallmouth. Although Dwight Webster of Cornell University found that even when alewives abounded and were the single most important food item for the smallmouth in Cayuga Lake, crayfish were a consistent part of the smallmouth diet. A seven-pound smallmouth that I kept in captivity for the better part of a year fed avidly on crayfish, but it never bothered a half dozen dace I placed in the tank with it. In fact, the bass allowed the dace to clean what appeared to be growths of fungus from around its mouth and flanks.

Smallmouths are far more sensitive to light than largemouths. During daylight hours, they are extraordinarily shelter oriented. In a series of experiments comparing the activity rhythms and light intensity preferences of the two species, William W. Reynolds and Martha E. Casterlin found that the morning peak activity of the largemouth occurred following the onset of light, while the morning activity of the smallmouth preceded the onset of light and declined sharply with the onset itself. The largemouth became active during midday, but the smallmouth did not. Both species became active in the evening, but the evening peaks were less pronounced than the morning peaks. A novel note: As part of the study, the fish were able to control a light switch. How they were able to do this is too technical to explain here, but the largemouth kept the light on 60 percent of the time while the smallmouth kept the light off 96 percent of the time.

Smallmouth bass in lakes tend to form discrete populations that do not stray far from home. William C. Latta, who tagged and released 3141 bass at Waugoschance Point in Lake Michigan, found that only eleven of them moved more than twenty miles during his three years of study. This strong tendency for smallmouth bass to restrict their range has been shown repeatedly in other bodies of water. John L. Forney found that about 80 percent of the recoveries of tagged fish in Oneida Lake, New York, were made within a mile and a half of the tagging site. Indeed, remarkably little exchange occurred between two populations which were separated by only three miles of open water. R. Weldon Larimore of the Illinois Natural History Survey found this home instinct in stream smallmouth so marked that fish may stay in the same pool for a season and those that are moved away from "home" will attempt to return. Given this, it is little wonder that fishermen can take a toll of some populations.

Although smallmouth bass are not supposed to thrive in

warm-water ponds, George Bennett and William Childers of the Illinois Natural History Survey showed that the fish were able to do so in a dozen ponds they stocked. Indeed, the smallmouth reproduced in half of them. Malcomson's Pond, a 1.4-acre body of water, was outstanding, even though the maximum depth was only twelve feet and the water was below average in relative fertility. The fish grew more rapidly than did smallmouth in Jordan Creek—they reached 11.1 inches by the end of the third growing season in the pond as compared to the 9.5 inches in the creek—and the fishing yields were higher than any previously reported for either smallmouth or largemouth. In 1952, the annual yield was 119.9 pounds per acre, and in 1953, 123 pounds per acre, prompting Bennett and Childers to report in "The Smallmouth Bass in Warm Water Ponds" that "it seems safe to assume that there may be an annual replacement of fish flesh which in this instance exceeds the standing crop that the pond will support." Smallmouth living by themselves in a pond become habitual surface feeders, and at Childer's Lake, another test pond, the two scientists collected fish not with a seine but with fly rods. In a total of twenty-two hours of fishing, mainly with small chartreuse poppers, they caught 192 smallmouth, an incredible catch rate average of almost nine fish per man-hour of fishing.

Childers is now working on a smallmouth-largemouth hybrid in an effort to find a fish that may have faster growth rates and more fighting ability than either parent. The first two generations of hybrids were nicknamed "Meanmouth" because they were, in Childers's words, "extremely aggressive and exhibited little, if any fear of man or other animals." He once watched a Meanmouth attack a woman swimmer. "The bass leaped from the water and struck her on her head and chest, and drove her from the pond," Childers reported to the First National Bass symposium. "She reentered the water approximately an hour later and the bass attacked her again." Another time, several Meanmouths ganged up on a dog in shallow water. "Several bass leaped out of the water and struck the dog. The dog repeatedly snapped at the bass but never caught one, and as the water in the area became muddy the bass abandoned their attack."

6/ The Striped Bass

There are largemouth bass up to five pounds in the Croton River in southern New York State, but anyone who fished for largemouth in the spring when I lived in Croton was considered out of his mind. Not when you had the chance to hook into a five-, ten-, fifteen-, or with luck a twenty-pound striped bass. In April the stripers surged into the river to gorge themselves on alewives and blueback herring in from the Atlantic to spawn. Up until June when the stripers moved out of the Croton and down the Hudson to saltwater along the coast, the action could be frantic. I caught 16 stripers one day and thought I was hot stuff until I ran into another fisherman who had taken 110 on plugs. He kept the three largest, nine pounds apiece, and then got greedy, returning the next day with a flat of bloodworms. He didn't get a touch. The striper is a hit-or-miss fish that is not a steady feeder. But when it feeds, so do other members of the school. In brief, the striper is a fish that can drive an angler wild with delight or frustration, but as a growing and enthusiastic army of largemouth fishermen across the country are now learning, the striper is becoming *the* trophy fish of many inland reservoirs.

Like the Atlantic salmon, the striped bass is a highly migratory anadromous fish native to the Atlantic coast of North America. (The striped bass in California and Oregon are the descendants of 435 small fish shipped across the country from New Jersey and planted in the San Francisco Bay area in 1879 and 1881.) Striped bass spend most of their adult lives in coastal salt water, but spawn in freshwater rivers which also provide nursery grounds for the young. As early as 1903 it was reported that striped bass would thrive in freshwater ponds if sufficiently fed, but no one had a glimmer of the remarkable freshwater potential of the striper until almost half a century later. In 1941, construction of the Santee-Cooper Reservoir in South Carolina trapped stripers that spawned upstream in rivers. The landlocked stripers spawned and flourished and became the source of a highly unusual and highly publicized freshwater sports fishery. South Carolina established an experimental hatchery at Moncks Corner where biologists were able to develop successful techniques for spawning and rearing striped bass for stocking elsewhere. Largely as the result of the work at Moncks Corner, more than thirty striper fisheries have developed in reservoirs in seventeen inland states, and there are naturally reproducing populations in Keystone Reservoir in Oklahoma, Kerr Reservoir in Virginia, Millerton Lake and the lower Colorado River in California, and Dardanelle Reservoir in Arkansas, among other locales.

Striped bass serve as an excellent fishery management tool in fresh water. They can reach extraordinary size feeding on the gizzard shad that have become too big for largemouth to engulf, and they often feed in the open waters of a reservoir, thus filling an ecological niche previously considered "dead" by fishermen. Wherever the striper and the largemouth coexist, the striper usually gets the nod from anglers. "In seven years of fishing for black bass in Lake Dardanelle and the Arkansas River, two eight-pounders were my largest fish," Terry Alexander of Little Rock told *Southern Outdoors*. "But after only 18 months of striper fishing at the same places, I've collected five over 10 pounds, including one which weighed 14 pounds three ounces." And of course there are fish that are larger. The present inland record is a fifty-nine-pound twelve-ounce striper taken in the Colorado River in 1977.

Although the striped bass is a rugged fighter, the fish cannot take physical handling the way a largemouth will. Striper eggs in a hatchery jar have died after being subjected to the flash from a photographer's camera. Indeed, it is possible to rupture an egg simply by stroking it with a single strand from a camel's-hair brush. Fingerlings have died from shock after the hatchery can "pinged" against the side of a truck, and boated adults will sometimes succumb to shock.

The scientific name for striped bass is *Morone saxatilis*, which means "stupid found among rocks." Until the 1960s *Roccus*, Latin doggerel for "rocks," was the generic name for the striper, but it was changed to *Morone* because that name had been used originally for the genus and therefore had priority under the rules of nomenclature. At about the same time taxonomists also shifted the striped bass and other members of the genus *Morone* from the Serranidae, the sea bass family, to the Percichthyidae, an obscure family that hitherto contained only one genus of South American freshwater fish. The shift was made because striped bass are not hermaphroditic as sea bass are, and because striped bass have only two spurs, not three, on the opercular bone near the gill. "Normally we would laugh at such things," says Dr. C. Lavett Smith of the American Museum of Natural History, a taxonomist who supported the switch, "but the change makes sense."

The spawning behavior of the striper is markedly different from that of the black bass. Spawning naturally occurs in rivers in the spring as the water temperatures move into the fifties. Males spawn starting at age two, the females at age four. The female broadcasts her eggs into the water where they are fertilized by a number of males which thrash around her. A number of males are apparently needed for spawning since the eggs are viable for only an hour. Because stripers do not guard their eggs, female stripers produce an enormous number of them. A ten-pounder produces about a million eggs and a fifty-pounder about five million. Striped bass of thirty pounds or more are almost always females. They live longer and grow to greater size. The scientific literature notes that females may live to be more than forty years old and reach 125 pounds.

The fertilized eggs drift with the current or move back and forth with the tides in an estuary. About 1.3 millimeters in diameter, the eggs are semi-buoyant, and moving water is necessary for their survival. Eggs can be found floating under the surface, at mid-depth, or toward the bottom of a river. Should they sink to the bottom and remain there, they will die; they must be free floating. As a general rule, in nontidal waters a downstream run of about fifty river miles or more is needed for egg development. Incubation takes about two days in water temperatures of 65 degrees and three days at 58 degrees.

After the eggs hatch, the young enter the larval stage. The larvae are slightly less than three millimeters long, and they are all but helpless as they move about with the current and tides. They feed themselves through the yolk sac because they lack a mouth opening for the first four to six days. By the time the young are three to four weeks old they are shaped like the adult fish and are silver in color. When two or three inches long, they bear parr marks of vertical stripes. When they reach four or five inches in length they assume the characteristic horizontal stripes of the adult.

The young are omnivorous feeders. The principal foods for those a third of an inch to an inch long are copepods, cladocerans, and insect larvae. When the young are longer than three and a half inches they begin to feed on fish.

In their natural habitat, adult bass consume a wide variety of organisms, including annelid worms, shrimps, crabs, squids, clams, mussels, herring, menhaden, mackerel, and eels, among others. (During the nineteenth century, lobster tails were a favorite bait with fishermen.) The fish has a well-developed sense of smell; one of the deadliest baits used in salt water is the smelly belly of a clam. Some inland fishermen have feared that the striper would prey on largemouth bass, but a two-year study by the Oklahoma Department of Wildlife Conservation at Keystone Reservoir disclosed that 84 percent of the striper diet consisted of gizzard shad. There were a few white crappies, but as biologist Dave Combs noted, "Of 467 striper stomachs examined at various times of the year, not a single black bass was found."

Striped bass offer fishermen still another advantage. In colder weather the fish do not cease feeding until the water temperature drops into the low forties, and they don't get the blahs that largemouth do during the dog days of summer. Stripers can be taken with streamers on a fly rod and by bait casting, but most freshwater angling is done with medium-heavy spinning tackle and artificials that suggest the gizzard shad. The most reliable fishing spots are directly below dams releasing water or generating power. The stripers line up like supermarket looters during a blackout waiting for the free goodies to come their way. Hair or feather jigs from two to six inches long are most productive. Diving plugs and silver spoons, such as the Hopkins, will also score but are used sparingly because of hangups.

Fishing an open lake is less predictable because the fish are harder to locate. Anglers often troll near old river or creek channels or keep an eye out for surface blitzes or gulls working the bait driven up from below. Most fishermen fish during the day, but striped bass often feed actively in the dark. Moreover, at night they dispense with caution and enter shallows to feed.

The rise of inland striper fishing comes, ironically enough, at a time when the species is in serious trouble in East Coast estuaries. At this writing, the stocks of striped bass along the Atlantic have plummeted to a dramatic low.

Various reasons have been advanced, among them pollution, especially chemical contamination, destruction of the eggs, larvae, and young by power plants that use estuarine water for cooling, and overfishing. Thanks to author John N. Cole, who wrote about the plight of the species in his book *Striper*, and to Sen. John Chafee of Rhode Island, who read it and acted, the federal government is about to embark on an intensive study of why the fish is in short supply. It just could be that should the Atlantic stocks need replenishment, the striped bass of inland waters are available as a source.

Here are some of the most successful or interesting old bass plugs in history, dating from 1876 to 1946, all gems from the Seth Rosenbaum Collection. Top left, Brush's Floating Wood Trolling Spoon (1876); bottom left, the Shakespeare Revolution (1902); top right, the Rush Tango (1917); bottom right, Dowagiac "150" (1920).

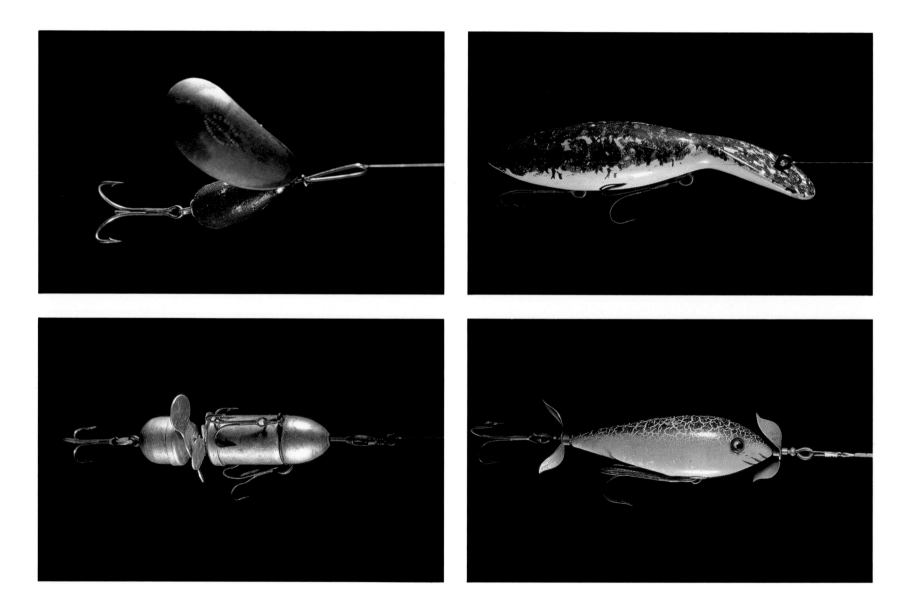

Top left, Louis Rhead's Crayfish (1922); bottom left, Carter's Best Ever (1925); top right, Little Luny Frog (1926); bottom right, Jointed Vamp (1930).

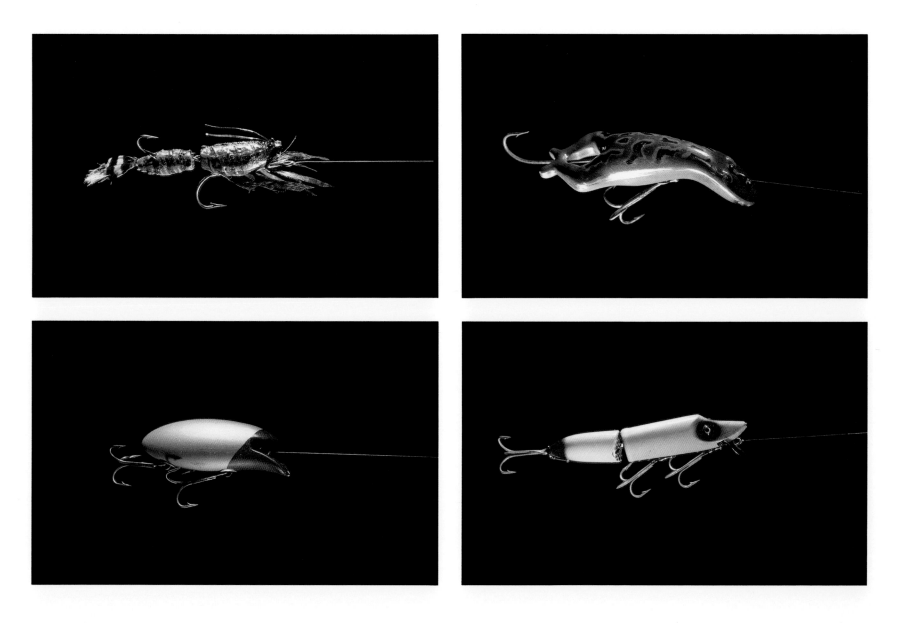

Top left, Barney Google (1935); bottom left, Whirl Oreno (1939); top right, Midget Popper (1943); bottom right, Peach Oreno (1946).

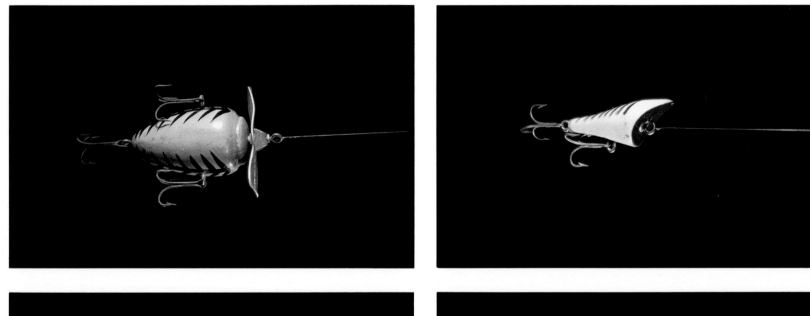

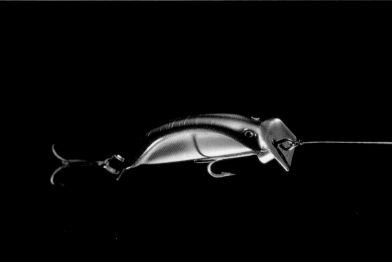

7/
Collecting
Vintage
Lures

In the last few years the collecting craze has seized Americans. From flea markets and antique shops to auction rooms, Americans are collecting a variety of objects, ranging from furniture to cigar cutters. Within the field of sporting collectibles alone, enthusiasts seek out guns, decoys, prints, knives, old ammunition, duck stamps, rods, reels, flies, and lures. Lure collecting is just beginning to burgeon.

The value of a lure depends on rarity and condition. For example, the ideal plug, at least from the collector's point of view, has never been used and comes in the original box. Most sell for five or ten dollars, but a very desirable plug, say a Heddon's slope-nosed Expert, has brought as much as $300. As more collectors pile in, the market is sure to soar. "Just a few years ago, less than 50 known collectors existed," says Seth Rosenbaum of Queens, New York. "Now that number is in the hundreds, with more still in the closet."

Rosenbaum should know: he is the most celebrated lure collector in the country. Housed in his apartment, his collection contains more than 12,000 lures, old tackle catalogues, books, and other ephemera to assist in research. A computer consultant by profession, Rosenbaum has been able to bring order out of what would otherwise be chaos by computerizing his lure collection on three master lists. These give the name of the lure, the date made, and the name of the manufacturer. The collection includes any number of nineteenth-century bass flies, which were taken from popular trout patterns of the period and fished wet. He also has a great number of bass bugs, ranging from Joe Messenger's popping bug and Zane Grey's creations (as fresh as the day they were made), to an experimental model of the Wilder-Dilg Feathered Minnow, accompanied by a note from Wilder's son detailing its development.

Rosenbaum also has an outstanding collection of flies and lures devised by Louis Rhead, a commercial artist who lived from 1857 to 1926. In 1916, Rhead published the first book of its kind in this country, *American Trout Stream Insects*, which included some of his very imaginative ties, but inasmuch as he gave his imitations fanciful names which beclouded entomological identification by anyone else, his work was dismissed—and has been dismissed—as that of an artistic dilettante. Yet Rhead's book *Fisherman's Lures and Game-fish Food*, published in 1920, and the frog, crayfish, and shiner imitations he sold under the name of "Nature Lures," show that he was far ahead of his time. Fishermen can learn from him even today. Rosenbaum obtained the bulk of his Rhead collection from the cellar of William Mills when that venerable Manhattan firm closed its downtown shop in 1971.

More than 7000 of Rosenbaum's 12,000 lures are plugs. Historically, plugs and bass are just about synonymous. Indeed, the record twenty-two-pound four-ounce largemouth fell for a Creek Chub Jointed Wag-Tail, while the record eleven-pound fifteen-ounce smallmouth glommed onto a white Bomber. Now in his forties, Rosenbaum began fishing when he was seven and he started collecting lures seriously

in his twenties. "Because of my business, I always traveled a great deal," he says, "and whenever I'd hit a town I'd head for the local tackle store. Tackle hadn't become as commercial as it is now. If a store didn't sell a plug in 1938, it was there in '39, and if it didn't sell in '39, it was there in '40. And it might still be there in '52 or '53. Dealers didn't clean out their shelves then—the stuff just stayed on forever. I found I could buy very old material that might have been around 15, 20, or 30 years. After the '50s, with new merchandising methods and everything in little plastic envelopes or blister packs, and with the price getting knocked down in 30, 60, or 90 days, it became harder and harder to find old tackle. I began to swap and advertise.

"Generally, I'll run an ad in a publication with a circulation of 40,000 or under. I don't want to get inundated. I've had trouble keeping up with the moderate amount of mail I receive. In Glens Falls, New York, I advertised in the daily paper once or twice. I did okay, maybe four or five responses. I got a Feather Gettum, which doesn't mean much to most people, but it's a rare lure. I also got a couple of old reels that I immediately passed on to Richard Miller in Hudson, Massachusetts, who collects reels, along with rods and some plugs. I'm waiting to see what I get back from him."

According to a hallowed story about the invention of the plug, one day in 1888 James Heddon, a Michigan bass fisherman, was whittling a piece of wood on Dowagiac Creek while waiting for a friend to come by. Idly, Heddon tossed the piece of wood into the creek and was astonished to see a largemouth belt it into the air. Idea! Whittling while he worked, Heddon started turning out "Dowjack" plugs for friends, and by 1902 business had grown to such proportions that he built the first factory to turn out plugs in volume.

A pretty story, but in Rosenbaum's archives, a copy of a 1921 issue of *The American Angler* contains an article, "Whence the Plug?" by Sam S. Stinson, in which Charles Heddon, son of James, is quoted as saying, "When asked who made the first wooden bait or plug, my father always used to exhibit two types of wooden minnows used by his grandfather in trolling for pickerel on Magician Lake, in this county, as far back as 1850 to 1855."

Actually, the first commercial plug, or what Rosenbaum says "could be considered the missing link between plugs and spinners," is the Floating Wood Trolling Spoon patented in 1876 by H. C. Brush. The first commercial Heddon plug was the Expert, sometimes known as the slope-nosed Expert because of the shape of the nose. "This is one of the rarest of the Heddons," Rosenbaum says. "Its rarity is exceeded only by the brass-mounted Underwater Expert."

The early Heddon plugs were made of cedar and invariably featured a propeller, as on the Artistic Minnow and the Double Dummy. Later plugs, such as the Deep O Diver, which is supposed to look like a crayfish, used a lip plate for diving. "Heddon specialized in hook gimmicks," says Rosenbaum. "His was the first company to come out with a hook hanger screwed into a plug. In 1911 Heddon introduced the Double Dummy, so called because of unusual hooks. Let me read

from an old ad: 'Jim Heddon's last invention, the Double Dummy design of hook, shows how triumphantly he satisfied his final ambition to produce a hook more certain of impaling the fish than any treble gang, yet free from its inhumanity and inconveniences.... The black bass, of all varieties and in all climates, always attacks the minnow at the side.... The single hook is placed to engage the upper jaw and the dummy portion comes into contact with the lower jaw, forcing the hook point into the upper jaw, without danger of disengagement.'"

Other companies sprang up to compete with Heddon: Creek Chub, South Bend, Pflueger, and Shakespeare (started by a man named William Shakespeare, Jr.). Each made contributions to the art of the plug ("The finishes on Shakespeare plugs were probably better than anyone else's," Rosenbaum says). The honor of manufacturing the first jointed minnow belongs to a small company, K & K, which was turning out its Animated Minnow by 1910.

"Many of the old plugs were outstanding fish catchers," Rosenbaum says. "I've received many pathetic letters from oldtime bass fishermen crying for specific baits no longer available in wood. I have also fished with most of the oldtime plugs in my collection, and some of them are extraordinary, truly extraordinary." If Rosenbaum had to rate the ten top bass plugs of all time, based on his considerable fishing experience with them, he would nominate the following:

The Rush Tango. "One of the greats, even though it was

made more than fifty years ago," Rosenbaum says. "The Tango floats when at rest, but almost half the plug is lip, and on a normal retrieve it dives to twenty-five feet, which is very deep indeed. That means that my line takes a really sharp angle in the water, and even as this floating plug goes down it has very nice action. If I stop reeling, buoyancy brings it up again, so that I have a kind of three-dimensional action working for me. Rush, who was in Utica, New York, also manufactured the Tiger Tango which has a blockier head than the regular Tango. The Tiger Tango is a great rarity."

Jim Donaly's Barney Google. Rosenbaum says, "In the '30s, a common response to the question 'What did you ketch 'em on?' was 'A Barney,' named after the comic strip character. It has a bulky body and a front propeller, and was a surface bait. It spins around when you retrieve it. It reappeared briefly as the Barney made by the McGagg Bait Company."

Vamp. "Every fisherman over sixty wants a wooden Vamp," says Rosenbaum. "They're desperate. I get requests all the time. Made by Heddon, it was one of the most popular plugs of all time. It was also made in plastic, but fishermen want it in wood. The original Vampire appeared in 1922, but the name was changed to Vamp in 1923."

Zaragossa. "Another immensely popular Heddon bait, it's still being made sporadically by Heddon in plastic, but veteran fishermen want it in wood. They consider the wooden model far superior in its swimming ability."

Midget Popper. Shakespeare produced this lure only in 1943. "It was ahead of its time as its quarter-ounce weight did not lend itself to bait casting," Rosenbaum says. "A great plug made of wood, and it's excellent now for spinning. The Midget Popper has two unique features. First of all, it stands upright in the water, head up and tail down, and second, its oversize lip makes a huge bubble and a wonderful commotion when the plug is popped."

Carter's Best Ever. "Charlie Fox, the well-known Pennsylvania angler and author, loves it," Rosenbaum says. "In Fox's words, 'There is built in the lure the potential for both enticing surface action, which can be produced by rod-tip manipulation, and for a realistic underwater swimming action, which can be produced by a fast retrieve. Thus, the angler controls both the lure's action and its swimming level.'"

Whirl Oreno. "South Bend made it and it's probably the best smallmouth plug I've ever used," Rosenbaum says. "The surface commotion, combined with the bucktail back, gets the bug-minded smallmouth to the surface."

Peach Oreno. "Another South Bend lure, the Peach Oreno might not look it, but it's made of solid brass, sinks like a stone, and is as fine a deep runner as you would want to use," Rosenbaum says. "Alas, as with all deep runners, the Peach Oreno can wind up stuck on the bottom. So all I can do with my remaining Peach Orenos is display them."

Waukazoo. "Shakespeare made this one, and with its pregnant body and bottom fin, it literally runs and takes small hops out of the water. It was manufactured in 1939 and was named after Waukegan, Illinois. Even if the Waukazoo doesn't catch a fish, just working it makes my day. But then it does take fish."

Luny Frog. "An underwater swimming frog and a very famous fish catcher," Rosenbaum says. "Made in two sizes, regular and little, by Heddon starting in 1926. To me, this is absolutely the greatest bass lure ever made. Fishing with a Luny Frog is like playing with a deck of marked cards. Most frog imitations float on the retrieve, but the Luny Frog comes back four or five feet underwater. Heddon made it of a material called Pyralin, similar to Bakelite, and that, alas, is both its strength and its weakness. If you cast a Luny Frog and hit a rock, you have an eighteen-piece Luny Frog." On rare occasions Rosenbaum will fish a Luny Frog with forty-pound test line after scouting an area to make certain there are no rocks in the vicinity. "I couldn't bear to lose a Luny Frog," he says. "They're very rare. They are very precious to me." When I once suggested with much throat clearing that I, ahem, would like, ahem, to borrow a Luny Frog, Rosenbaum raised a hand in caution and said, "My dear fellow, you can move into my apartment for a week, eat all the food in my well-stocked larder, run up a huge phone bill, give wild parties, and carry on in general, but I'll be in a motel, along with every Luny Frog I own."

Mentally, Rosenbaum passes many of his idle hours living in the years 1910 and 1911, which he fondly refers to as "the Golden Age of Plugs, when everybody was getting into the act." On occasion he will attempt to make that Golden Age come true. A couple of years ago, for example, Rosenbaum arrived at my house for some bass fishing. He was toting an ancient leather tackle box containing everything but a sled named *Rosebud.* There were antique bait-casting reels with braided silk lines, quill minnows from Victorian England, a selection of snelled-catgut hooks, and, of course, a generous selection of vintage plugs. Out on a local pond, Rosenbaum tied on a Rush Tango and let fly. On his third cast, a twelve-inch bass struck. "Camera! Camera!" he cried. "One doesn't see this every day!" Upon releasing the bass, Rosenbaum confided, "What I've always wanted to have happen is to be fishing and have some stranger ask me, 'Hey, bud, what works on this lake?' And I'll casually answer, 'Oh, the 1902 Shakespeare Revolution and the 1917 Rush Tango are favorites here.'"

8/
On Tying Flies and Making Lures

Tying bass flies and bugs and making lures is one of the most pleasant pastimes known to the serious angler. It is a marvelous way of passing the winter or using spare time. Whenever I go on an assignment or a pleasure trip, I always take along a vise, hooks, and assorted materials in a portable kit because I am then never at a loss for something to do. I remember a trip to Florida when Sonny Werblin, who used to run the Jets and now presides over Madison Square Garden, kept postponing his interview with me. Inasmuch as I had to stay in my hotel room waiting for him to call when he was free, the trip would have been a disaster had I not passed the hours blissfully concocting a new version of a feathered bass bug. The bass fisherman who does not tie his own flies or make his own jigs is missing a great deal of enjoyment, not only in tying or just *thinking* about what to tie, but in fishing itself. The advantages are several. For one, the fisherman who buys bugs is usually cautious when afield. "Should I cast this bug into that thick tangle of lily pads?" he asks himself. "No, I might lose it, and it cost me two bucks." This fiscal conservative moves to unproductive open water and flails away without success. By contrast, the bug tier will have no hesitancy about casting into the thickest cover. If he loses a bug, he has a dozen more in hand, and should he lose those as well, he can always tie more at the cost of a few cents each.

Another advantage, and a most important one, in tying your own is that you can design them to do a specific job or to meet a certain situation. You don't have this leeway if you are dependent on tackle shops. I recall fishing a small, weed-choked pond that had a goodly number of bass, but to get to them I had to have a bug that would sink quickly, be of a good size, be weedless, and have action. Accordingly I came up with a huge yellow deer-hair and saddle-hackle monster that was both weighted and weedless. A cross between a bug and a plug, this "blug" described later, did the job most satisfactorily.

The Kat's Meow Streamer-Jig

The simplest tie I know is the most effective. It is called the Kat's Meow, and if I had to be restricted to only one lure for the rest of my life, I would pick the Kat's Meow without hesitation. It has caught largemouth and smallmouth bass, striped bass, trout, jack crevalle, white perch, crappies, sunfish, herring—you name it. It has one drawback: because it is so small, you will get more than your share of panfish rather than bass, but if you're prepared to put up with the sunnies, you'll get your bass as well. Moreover, it can be used to effect on sophisticated fish. The Kat's Meow met Seth Rosenbaum's ultimate test. He used it in a Catskill lake to catch the largemouths that hung out next to a boat pier. All summer long, these wary fish had ignored every lure cast their way by fishermen, but Rosenbaum took them bang, bang, bang. All in all, it is such a deadly lure that I make it barbless so I can quickly release the fish I don't want. I use the Kat's Meow on a fly rod or on an ultralight spinning rod with two- or four-pound test line. With its head of small split-shot, the Kat's Meow can dip and dart like a small minnow feeding on the bottom or crawl along like a nymph. Because of the way the split-shot head is placed, the point of the hook rises rightside up to prevent snagging. Even when stuffed full, a bass will pounce upon the enticing Kat's Meow like a fat person who just can't resist that last little piece of fudge.

Hook: Size 10, Mustad 94833, dry fly. (I prefer the dry-fly hook because it is made of finer wire than the wet-fly hook and has better penetrating qualities.)

Thread: Herb Howard's or Danville's prewaxed black.

Head: Split-shot, painted black after the Kat's Meow is tied. (Eyes are optional, but I believe they add to the effectiveness of the Kat's Meow.)

Body: None.

Tail: Rabbit hair dyed black. Several strands of fine (1/64th-inch-width) silver mylar may be added.

2. Tie in the black rabbit hair directly behind the split-shot. To avoid lumpiness and to allow the hair to have full play when fished, try to use as few turns of the thread as possible to secure the hair. If you wish, tie in several strands of fine mylar on top of the hair. The mylar helps simulate the silver underbelly of a bait fish. Tie off with a whip finish and apply a dab of clear lacquer to the binding.

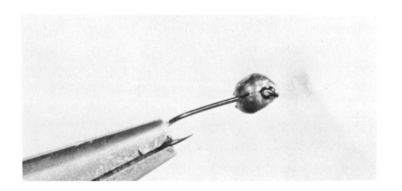

1. Press the split-shot on the hook immediately behind the eye with needle-nose pliers. Be sure to place the split-shot on as shown so that the hook will ride rightside up. If you're going to be making a dozen or more Kat's Meows, it saves time to press the heads on them all at one time. Insert the hook in the vise as shown, with the point down. Wrap the tying thread three times around the shank directly behind the split-shot.

3. Remove the Kat's Meow from the vise and give the head two coats of black lacquer. To form the eyes, dip the tip of a small round dowel into white or yellow lacquer and touch it to both sides of the split-shot to make the irises. To make the pupils, use the tip of a smaller round dowel dipped in black lacquer and touch it to the middle of each iris.

All sorts of variations can be tied. Instead of using white hen hackles, you can try feather whisks of other colors or long, soft fur. Rabbit hair, dyed black, makes an excellent imitation of a fingerling catfish or a nymph. Indeed, you can match almost any fish or nymph.For instance, I imitate baby pumpkinseed sunfish with whisks of blue and orange hackle mixed with a few strands of fine gold mylar, and I then paint the head blue. Wood duck or mallard breast feathers can be used to imitate the color and scales of a darter.

While I was experimenting with various furs, I tied the fur nymphs shown here. Instead of using a split-shot to weight the head, I wrapped fuse wire around the length of the shank and then tied in fur which undulates and breathes in the water. I have used the fur nymph with success on small-mouths simply by jigging it up and down rock ledges.

The Deer-Hair Bug

The classic bass bug is tied with the body hair of a white-tailed deer. The hair is hollow so it floats well. When tied on a hook shank, it flares easily and can be trimmed to imitate a variety of animals, ranging from a moth to a mouse. The back and side hairs on the hide of a deer are brown at the tips and gray on the butts, while the belly hair is white and readily takes a dye. Yellow, red, orange, and black are favorite colors for bugs. Here is a yellow moth.

Hook: Size 1.
Body: Yellow deer body hair.
Thread: Size D, yellow nylon, waxed.

1. Size D nylon is strong enough to stand the strain of tying a big deer-hair bug. Be sure to wax the thread by drawing it through tying wax, otherwise the thread will slip and slide on the hook shank.

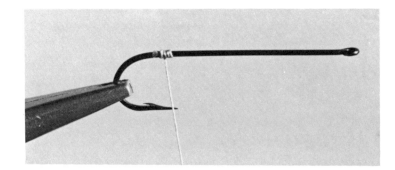

2. Insert the hook in the vise and wrap the tying thread over itself three or four times near the bend of the hook. Cut off the excess thread. A spool of size D thread is too big for a bobbin, so make sure that the thread is held under tension. I generally use a pair of hackle pliers to do this.

3. Snip a bunch of deer hair, about the thickness of a soda straw, off the hide. Hold it parallel to the shank and take two or three turns of the tying thread around it.

4. The pressure of the tying thread causes the hair to flare. By making additional turns of thread around the hair, you can get it to flare more evenly than shown here.

5. Continue tying on hair until it extends to just behind

the eye of the hook. Tie off the tying thread and put a drop of clear lacquer on the thread head.

6. Remove the bug from the vise and trim to shape with scissors. The finished moth.

You can trim the bug to almost any shape. By adding yellow bucktail to the tail of a bullet-shaped bug, I made the floating top minnow shown here. The "blug" to which I referred

earlier is also shown. To make it, I simply wrapped fuse wire around the shank for weight, then I tied in the hair. The unclipped hair before the point of the hook serves as both an imitation fin and a weed guard, and the feathers tied in at the tail give the blug undulating movement underwater. The first time I used it in heavy weeds, I was fast to a four-pound bass.

Quill Stub Dragonfly

At first, I used to spend up to two hours tying a realistic dragonfly. Talk about super-realism. I would only tie with natural materials obtained locally, such as quill stubs from a Canada goose and horse hair (for the wings) from a nearby neighbor, and then I would only imitate species of dragonflies found in the ponds I fished. I recall devising a very realistic imitation of *Anax junius,* the big "King of June" dragonfly. This imitation not only caught bass, but I was able to capture the living insect itself, which is ordinarily extremely wary, simply by dangling the imitation off the end of my fly rod while a friend netted *Anax* when it flew in either to kill or to mate with my concoction.

Although I do love to devote hours to tying the ultimate fly or bug, I have now cut the tying time of the dragonfly to ten minutes to do a rough imitation. It's realistic enough all right, at least enough to catch fish, and that's what counts.

Hook: Size 8 streamer hook.
Tying thread: Herb Howard's or Danville's prewaxed red.
Body: Abdomen and basic thorax are the transparent end stub of a Canada goose or peacock quill dyed red.
Thorax: Mixture of rabbit fur and wool dyed red.
Wings: Four long neck hackles.

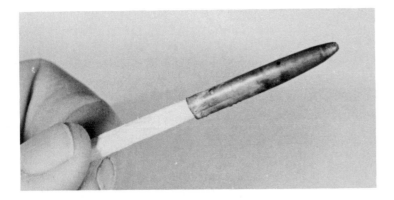

1. Insert a piece of balsa wood, freshly lacquered with fingernail polish, inside the dyed quill stub. This will help keep the quill stub from turning and also adds to the floatability.

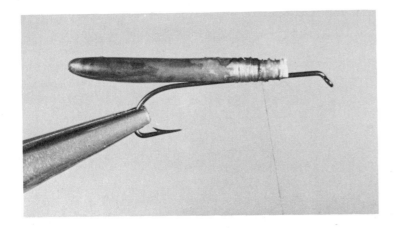

2. Tie a dozen or so wraps of the tying thread around the protruding piece of balsa wood to secure the quill stub to the shank.

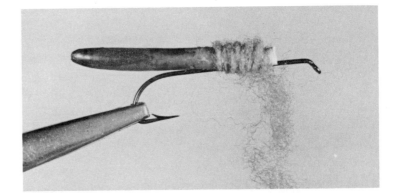

3. Cover the wrappings and build up the thorax with a mixture of rabbit fur and wool dyed red. To get the fur and wool mixture to adhere to the tying thread, apply fingernail polish to the thread to make it tacky, then "spin" on the fur and hair mixture by rolling it between your fingers in the shape of a noodle.

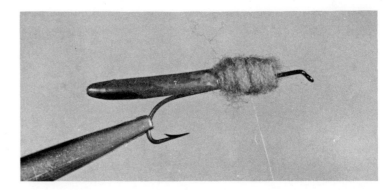

4. The finished thorax. I am now ready to tie in four feathers as the wings.

6. The finished dragonfly from the bass's point of view.

5. A cheap hen neck has feathers that make ideal wings for the dragonfly. Select four of them. The hind pair should be longer than the front pair. The wings tied on top of the thorax. Getting the wings to plane correctly can be trying, but the fur-wool thorax mixture helps give purchase so the feathers will not slip out of place. The fur-wool mixture is added to serve as the head.

If you wish, you can add dark rubber strands for the six legs. Sometimes I'm a leg man, sometimes I'm not. But if you do use legs, rubber gives the dragonfly that extra twitch of life when moved in the water.

Also shown here is a very realistic dragonfly I tied. I used India ink to simulate the body markings. I set it in the vise to put on new wings of looped horsehair. The old ones finally gave way after twelve years of fishing. The thorax, by the way, is made of deer body hair clipped to shape and lacquered, and the legs are of javelina hair.

Also shown here is a quill-body minnow, a miniature plug for the fly rod. Just tie the quill stub on the hook (with balsa wood inside), add eyes, and fish.

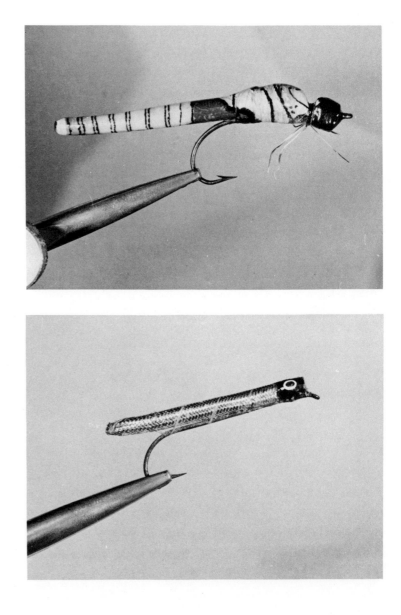

The Grass Shrimp

Here is a fly to dazzle the eye of both fish and fishermen. I originally tied it to catch striped bass in the Croton River, and it has since gone on to take largemouths, smallmouths, rainbow trout, browns, brook trout, Atlantic salmon, weak fish, mackerel, white perch, and assorted panfish. In the August 1976 issue of *Field & Stream*, Eric Peper chose this shrimp as the "Fly of the Month" and called it "a work of art, or as perfect an imitation of a natural fish food as it is possible to make." I don't want to seem immodest, but this shrimp is so lifelike that it's often stolen when exhibited. I don't like thieves, but to a fly tier theft has to be the ultimate compliment. The shrimp appears complicated to tie, but it really is not. The trick is in using the right materials, such as transparent tying thread, so the actual tying does not show.

Hook: Mustad wide-gap bait hook, sizes 2 down to 12.
Thread: Dyno transparent sewing thread.
Body: Clear strips of a plastic known as Clorpane and K-Clear. This is ordinarily sold in variety stores in large sheets that are used to cover typewriters, lampshades, and other office or household articles to keep off dust.
Small antennae: Half a dozen or so Polar bear hairs, fine ends forward.
Long antennae: Two clear hog bristles.
Lip plates: Clear quill cut from the end stub of a Canada goose or peacock quill and trimmed to shape.

Nose or rostrum: Clear quill trimmed to shape.
Eyes: Two bulbous ends of chicken feathers tipped with black lacquer, or twenty- to forty-pound test monofilament burned at the ends as shown.
Legs: The butt ends of the small antennae of Polar bear hairs brought forward.

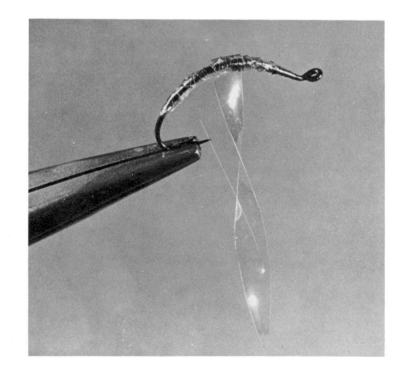

1. Tie in a narrow strip of Clorpane; then spiral it around the hook over itself to build up a tapered body.

2. Secure the Clorpane wrappings in place with the Dyno transparent thread, coat it with clear fingernail polish, and then put the body in the vise upside down. Wind the thread toward the eye to tie in the Polar bear hairs that represent the shrimp's small antennae. Do not trim the butts of the hairs because they will later serve as the legs.

3. Trim the lip plates from quill stub, place them over the wrappings securing the small antennae and tie down. Coat with fingernail polish.

4. Take two long bristles and tie them down over the lip plates.

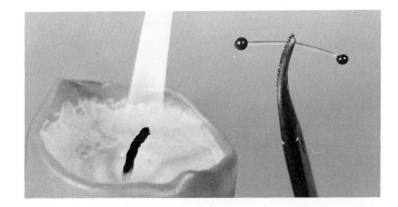

5. Put the shrimp in the vise rightside up and tie in the eyes. The eyes can be made from monofilament by touching the ends to a flame, as shown here, but in this case I have used the

bulbous ends of two feathers. Tie them in on both sides with the transparent tying thread, and again coat with fingernail polish. Later you can dab black lacquer on the tips of the eyes, as I have done here so the eyes stand out in the photograph. Tie in the nose or rostrum, trimmed to a point, point forward over the eye. Coat the thread with fingernail polish.

6. Remove the shrimp from the vise and place upside down. Now bring the butt ends of the Polar bear hairs forward and use the tying thread to hold them in that position. Tie off and coat with fingernail polish.

7. Remove the shrimp from the vise and coat it lightly with fingernail polish. This adds to the luster and transparency. Coat again, let dry, then coat still again. The coatings of polish will fill up any ridges in the body and give the tied shrimp added lifelike appearance. Here is a shrimp I tied with bent legs and down pleopods.

Stuempfig's Painted Turtle

This imaginative spinning lure was devised by Anthony A. P. Stuempfig, a well-known Philadelphia antique dealer who specializes in masterpieces of nineteenth-century American furniture. He is also a dedicated bass nut, and when he isn't dealing in Duncan Phyfe, he's tying bugs, making lures, and turning out his own rods.

Hook: Wright & McGill No. 1 weedless.
Body: Hammered Colorado spinner blade.

Take the spinner blade and place it on the workbench so the saucer-shaped side faces up. Set the hook upside down, so the point rides up, in the curve of the long axis of the blade. Hold the hook in place with surgical clamps. Solder the hook shank to the blade behind the eye and before the bend. Stuempfig applies a few drops of soldering acid, heats with a soldering iron, and then applies sixty-forty solder—60 percent tin and 40 percent lead, this solder is very strong. Now paint the hook shank and the concave side of the blade black. Turn over the blade and paint it as shown here so that it resembles the plastron (belly) of a hatchling painted turtle. The final step is to drill a hole through the blade matching the eye of the hook.

Stuempfig invented the lure several years ago one June when he made a stomach examination of some largemouth bass from a reservoir and found that they had been eating hatchling turtles as they entered the water from a cove. When cast, the turtle lure rides hook-side up, allowing the fisherman to crawl it across lily pads, rocks, and logs. In the water, it wobbles like mad. Sometimes Stuempfig attaches a black pork-rind tail to the hook to give the turtle enough weight to make it sink quickly in the holes between lily pads. "The weight also keeps the spinner blade pointed up so it doesn't foul in heavy weeds," he says. "Bass just try to kill it." He finds it most effective during a two-week period in June when the turtles are hatching, but adds that the belly can be painted to match the plastron on any species of turtle that has just hatched.

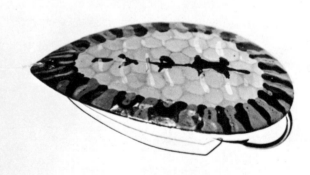

9/
Bass
for the
Table

Except when tagging bass for study, I keep every bass I catch of legal size from clean waters. I make it a point to fillet every fish for the table because one bone can spoil a meal. I have no desire to add to the world's larder of recipes, but here are three for bass that are simple, different, and delicious.

CHILLED BASS

Cut the fillets into two-inch-long chunks and drop them into salted boiling water for two minutes. Remove, drain, place in a jar, and put in the refrigerator to cool. When chilled, serve the chunks with cocktail sauce (the bass will remind you of shrimp or lobster) or a light mustard, dill, hollandaise, or mousseline sauce. If you wish, you can flake the chilled fillets and serve in a salad or use on a sandwich.

BASS KATYA

Slice fresh tomatoes into inch-thick slices and place them on aluminum foil. Sprinkle with freshly ground pepper, freshly minced garlic, salt, and oregano, dust with bread crumbs, and top with a thin pat of butter. Put a chunk of fillet on top of this and place it in the broiler until the tomato is cooked through and the fish flakes. Remove, place a slice of thinly sliced Swiss cheese on top of the fish, and return it to the broiler briefly until the cheese starts to melt. Remove and serve this versatile dish either as an appetizer or dinner.

PICKLED BASS

Place eight to a dozen fillets in a brine solution, one-quarter salt, for two days. Remove and rinse the fillets of salt in cold water. Take a quart jar and line the bottom with thinly sliced onion. Add several peppercorns, one-eighth teaspoon of oregano, two bay leaves, several sprigs of fresh parsley, a quarter teaspoon of thyme, three stalks of chopped celery, and several dashes of Tabasco sauce. Place a layer of fillets on top of these. Cover this layer of fillets with finely sliced onion, add another layer of fillets, cover with onion, and so on until the jar is full. Pour in a solution of half wine vinegar and half water, and fill to the brim. Put the lid on the jar, place the jar in the refrigerator, and serve a week later.

Bibliography

The reader seeking to pursue further information about points and issues raised in this book should consult the following books and papers I used.

CHAPTER 1

The basic book on bass is *Black Bass, Biology and Management*, compiled by Richard H. Stroud and Henry Clepper, and published by the Sport Fishing Institute in Washington, D.C. in 1975. It contains all the papers delivered at the First National Bass Symposium. Especially valuable are "Life History and Biology of the Largemouth Bass" by Roy C. Heidinger, "Smallmouth Bass" by Daniel W. Coble, "Taxonomic History and Systematic Relationships Among Species of Micropterus" by John S. Ramsey, "Distribution of the Black Basses in North America" by Hugh R. MacCrimmon and William H. Robbins, "Black Bass Crops and Species Associations in Reservoirs" by Robert M. Jenkins, "Relationship Between Weather and Year-Class Strength of Largemouth Bass" by Robert C. Summerfelt, "Dynamics of Bass in Large Natural Lakes" by William C. Latta, "Factors Influencing the Quality of Largemouth Bass Fishing" by Richard C. Anderson, "Environmental Influences on the Mortality of Bass Embryos and Larvae" by Alfred W. Eipper, and "Bass Genetics as Applied to Culture and Management" by William F. Childers. Roy C. Heidinger is also the author of *An Indexed Bibliography of the Largemouth Bass, Micropterus salmoides (Lacépède)*, published in 1974 by the Fisheries Research Laboratory and Department of Zoology, Southern Illinois University. Victor A. Cvancara of the Department of Biology of the University of Wisconsin at Eau Claire compiles and publishes an annual bibliography, *Current References in Fish Research*. So far, three volumes have appeared, covering the years 1976, 1977, and 1978.

For the evolution and behavior of fishes in general, see Brian Curtis, *The Life Story of the Fish* (New York, 1949); Karl F. Lagler, John E. Bardach, and Robert R. Miller, *Ichthyology* (New York, 1962); J. R. Norman, *A History of Fishes* (2nd edition by P. H. Greenwood; New York, 1963); and Mark Sosin and John Clark, *Through the Fish's Eye* (New York, 1973).

Life-history data on the largemouth bass and the other centrarchid fishes is to be found in Kenneth D. Carlander's *Handbook of Freshwater Fishery Biology*, volume 2 (Ames, Iowa, 1977).

Carl L. Hubbs and Reeve M. Bailey discuss the distinguishing characteristics of the Centrarchidae in "The Small-Mouthed Bass," Bulletin No. 10 of the Cranbrook Institute of Science, January 1938. See also C. Lavett Smith and Reeve M. Bailey, "Evolution of the Dorsal-Fin Supports of Percoid Fishes," Papers of the Michigan Academy of Science, Arts, and Letters, 46, (1961); Hubbs and Bailey, "A Revision of the Black Basses (*Micropterus* and *Huro*) with Descriptions of Four New Forms," Miscellaneous Publications, No. 48, Museum of Zoology, University of Michigan, 1940; and Bailey and Hubbs, "The Black Basses (*Micropterus*) of Florida with Description of a New Species," Occasional Papers of the Museum of Zoology, No. 516, University of Michigan, 1949.

The history of fishing, including bass fishing, is dealt with by Erhard Rostlund, *Freshwater Fish and Fishing in Native North America*, University of California Publications in Geography, volume 9 (Berkeley and Los Angeles, 1952); Charles Eliot Goodspeed,

Angling in America (Boston, 1939), from which I have drawn the quotations by the editor of the *Turf Register*, Kit Clarke and Charles Hallock; Thaddeus Norris, *The American Angler's Book* (Memorial Edition; Philadelphia, 1865); and, of course, James A. Henshall, *Book of the Black Bass* (new edition, revised and extended; Cincinnati, 1904). For a discussion of fish stocking in the West, see H. M. Smith, "A Review of the History and Results of the Attempts to Acclimate Fish and Other Water Animals to the Pacific States," *Bulletin of the United States Fish Commission*, 1895 (Washington, D.C., 1896), and for the stocking of bass abroad, see William H. Robbins and Hugh R. MacCrimmon, *The Black Bass in America and Overseas* (Sault Ste. Marie, Ontario, 1974) and A. Cecil Harrison, *Black Bass in the Cape Province* (Pretoria, 1936), which has an account of bass in Kenya.

For the development of bass stocking and management, see Henry A. Regier, "On the Evolution of Bass-Bluegill Stocking Policies and Management Recommendations," *The Progressive Fish Culturist*, July 1962; Norman G. Benson, *A Century of Fisheries in North America*, Special Publication No. 7, American Fisheries Society (Washington, 1970); David G. Frey, ed., *Limnology in North America* (Madison, Wisc., 1965); Harlow B. Mills et al., "A Century of Biological Research," *Illinois Natural History Survey Bulletin* (December 1958); and George W. Bennett, *Management of Lakes and Ponds* (2nd edition; New York, 1971). For an account of the dismal fate of a once-great bass river, see Harlow B. Mills, William C. Starrett, and Frank C. Bellrose, "Man's Effect on the Fish and Wildlife of the Illinois River," Illinois Natural History Survey Biological Notes No. 57, 1966.

CHAPTER 2

For spawning, see C. M. Breder, Jr., "The Reproductive Habits of the North American Sunfishes (Family Centrarchidae)," *Zoologica* 21, pt. 1, nos. 1 and 2 (1936); Don Hunnsaker II and R. W. Crawford, "Preferential Spawning Behavior of the Largemouth Bass, *Micropterus salmoides*," *Copeia*, no. 1, 1964; Marjorie H. Carr, "The Breeding Habits, Embryology and Larval Development of the Largemouthed Black Bass in Florida," *Proceedings of the New England Zoological Club*, 20 (1942); and W. F. Carbine, "Observations on the Spawning Habits of Centarchid Fishes in Deep Lake, Oakland County, Michigan," *Transactions of the Fourth North American Wildlife Conference* (1939).

For the Cornell University research, see Clarence A. Carlson, "Life and Death in the Largemouth Bass," *The Conservationist*, August-September 1969, pp. 20–1; M. J. Shealy, Jr., "Nesting Bass Observed with Underwater Television," *New York's Food and Life Sciences* 4, no. 4 (October-December 1971): 18–20; James W. Eckblad and M. H. Shealy, Jr., "Predation on Largemouth Bass Embryos by the Pond Snail Viviparus georgianus," *Transactions of the American Fisheries Society* 101, no. 4 (October 1972): 734–8; Geoffrey C. Laurence, "The Energy Expenditure of Largemouth Bass Larvae, *Micropterus salmoides*, during Yolk Absorption," *Transactions of the American Fisheries Society* 98, no. 3 (July 1969); Laurence, "Digestion Rate of Larval Bass," *New York Fish and Game Journal* 18, no. 1 (1971); and Clarence A. Carlson and M. H. Shealy, Jr, "Marking Larval Largemouth Bass with Radiostrontium," *Journal of the Fisheries Research Board of Canada* 29, no. 4 (1972).

Other papers of note are Robert H. Kramer and Lloyd L. Smith, Jr., "Formation of Year Classes in Largemouth Bass," *Transactions of the American Fisheries Society* 91, no. 1 (1962); Gerald P. Cooper, "Food Habits, Rate of Growth and Cannibalism of Young Largemouth Bass (*Aplites salmoides*) in State-Operated Rearing Ponds in Michigan during 1935," *Transactions of the American Fisheries Society* 66 (1936); Henry C. Markus, "The Extent to Which Temperature Changes Influence Food Consumption in Largemouth Bass (*Huro floridana*)," *Transactions of the American Fisheries Society* 62 (1932); Gyula Molnár and István Tölg, "Relation Between Water Temperature and Gastric Digestion of Largemouth Bass (*Micropterus salmoides* Lacépède)," *Journal of the Fisheries Research Board of Canada* 19, no. 6 (1962).

For dragonflies, see Charles Branch Wilson, "Dragonflies and Damselflies in Relation to Pondfish Culture," *Bulletin of the Bureau of Fisheries* 36 (1917–8); and Philip S. Corbet, *A Biology of Dragonflies* (London, 1962).

CHAPTER 3

For aspects of feeding, see Allen Keast and Deirdre Webb, "Mouth and Body Form Relative to Feeding Ecology in the Fish Fauna of a Small Lake, Lake Opinicon, Ontario," *Journal of the Fisheries Research Board of Canada* 23, no. 12 (1966); and William M. Lewis, Gerald E. Gunning, Edward Lyles, and W. Leigh Bridges, "Food Choice of Largemouth Bass as a Function of Availability and Vulnerability of Food Items," *Transactions of the American Fisheries Society* 90, no. 3 (1961).

A very important paper is Frank A. Brown, Jr., "Responses of the Largemouth Black Bass to Colors," *Illinois Natural History Survey Bulletin* 21 (1937). For the homing instinct, see Arthur D. Hasler and Warren J. Wisby, "The Return of Displaced Largemouth Bass and Green Sunfish to a 'Home' Area," *Ecology* 39, no. 2 (1958).

For parasites, disease, and pollution, see George W. Hunter III, "Studies on the Parasites of Fresh-Water Fishes of Connecticut," *A Fishery Survey of Important Connecticut Lakes* (Hartford, 1942); H. S. Davis, *Culture and Diseases of Game Fishes* (Berkeley and Los Angeles, 1961); Stanislas F. Snieszko, ed., *A Symposium on Diseases of Fishes and Shellfishes* (Washington, D.C., 1970), Special Publication No. 5 of the American Fisheries Society; and the Environmental Defense Fund and Robert H. Boyle, *Malignant Neglect* (New York, 1979), which deals with known or suspected cancer-causing agents in the environment, including PCBs.

CHAPTER 4

See George W. Bennett's *Management of Lakes and Ponds*, previously cited in the bibliography for Chapter 1. Other Bennett papers of importance are "The Growth of the Large Mouthed Black Bass, *Huro salmoides* (Lacépède), in the Waters of Wisconsin," *Copeia*, no. 2, August 18, 1937; "Management of Small Artificial Lakes," *Bulletin of the Illinois Natural History Survey* 22 (1943); "Overfishing in a Small Artificial Lake," *Bulletin of the Illinois Natural History Survey* 23 (1945); "Largemouth Bass in Ridge Lake, Coles County, Illinois," *Bulletin of the Illinois Natural History Survey* 26 (1954); "Aquatic Biology" in "A Century of Biological Research," *Illinois Natural History Survey Bulletin* 27 (1958); "The Environmental Requirements of Centrarchids with Special Reference to Largemouth Bass, Smallmouth Bass, and Spotted Bass," *Biological Problems in Water Pollution*, Third Seminar, August 13–17, 1962, U.S. Department of Health, Education and Welfare, Public Health Service Publication No. 999–WP–25; "Largemouth Bass and Other Fishes in Ridge Lake, Illinois, 1941–1963" (written with H. Wickliffe Adkins and William F. Childers), *Illinois Natural History Survey Bulletin* 30 (1969); also with Adkins and Childers, "The Effects of Supplemental Feeding and Fall Drawdowns on the Largemouth Bass and Bluegills at Ridge Lake, Illinois," *Illinois Natural History Survey Bulletin* 31 (1973); and "Ecology and Management of Largemouth Bass" in *Symposium on Overharvest and Management of Largemouth Bass in Small Impoundments*, edited by John L. Funk, North Central Division, American Fisheries Society Special Publication No. 3, 1974. In addition, I had the benefit of personal discussions and correspondence with Bennett from 1962 until shortly before his death in 1977.

See also Robert J. Schoffman, "Age and Rate of Growth of the Largemouth Black Bass in Reelfoot Lake, Tennessee, for 1952 and 1961," *Journal of the Tennessee Academy of Science* 37, no. 1 (1962).

CHAPTER 5

Hubbs and Bailey's *The Small-Mouthed Bass*, previously cited, is the best single book, but see also Daniel W. Coble's paper in *Black Bass, Biology and Management*. Also of importance are Dwight A. Webster, "Smallmouth Bass, *Micropterus dolomieui*, in Cayuga

Lake. I. Life History and Environment," Memoir 327, Cornell University Agricultural Experiment Station, 1954; and William C. Latta, "The Life History of the Smallmouth Bass, *Micropterus d. dolomieui*, at Waugoshance Point, Lake Michigan," *Bulletin of the Institute for Fisheries Research*, no. 5, Michigan Department of Conservation (no date but largely drawn from a doctoral dissertation submitted to the University of Michigan in 1957).

For feeding, see Albert L. Tester, "Food of the Small-Mouthed Black Bass (*Micropterus dolomieui*) in Some Ontario Waters," *University of Toronto Studies*, Publications of the Ontario Fisheries Research Laboratory, no. 46, 1932.

Other studies of interest are John L. Forney, "Growth, Movements and Survival of Smallmouth Bass (*Micropterus dolomieui*) in Oneida Lake, New York," *New York Fish and Game Journal* 8, no. 2 (1961); Udell B. Stone, Donald G. Pasko, and Robert M. Roecker, "A Study of Lake Ontario–St. Lawrence River Smallmouth Bass," *New York Fish and Game Journal* 1, no. 1 (1954); R. Weldon Larimore, "Bass Stocked in a Warm-Water Stream," *Journal of Wildlife Management* 18, no. 2 (1954); George W. Bennett and William F. Childers, "The Smallmouth Bass, *Micropterus dolomieui*, in Warm-Water Ponds," *Journal of Wildlife Management* 21, no. 4 (1957); and William E. Reynolds and Martha E. Casterlin, "Activity Rhythm and Light Intensity Preferences of *Micropterus salmoides* and *M. dolomieui*," *Transactions of the American Fisheries Society* 105, no. 3 (1976).

For an angler's account, see Billy Westmorland, as told to Larry Mayer, *Ol' Brown Fish* (Nashville, 1976).

Elizabeth D. Woodbury compiled "The Smallmouth Bass (*Micropterus dolomieui*), An Annotated and Selected Bibliography," Bibliography Series No. 32, March 1975, for the Natural Resources Library of the U.S. Department of the Interior.

CHAPTER 6

The literature on striped bass in estuarine and coastal waters is voluminous, but far less so for stripers in freshwater impoundments. However, freshwater fishermen can profit from reading papers and books on stripers in coastal waters. See Edward C. Raney, Ernest F. Tresselt, Edgar H. Hollis, V. D. Vladykov, and D. H. Wallace, "The Striped Bass," *Bulletin of the Bingham Oceanographic Collection* (Peabody Museum of Natural History, Yale University) 14 (1952). Raney's paper "The Life History of the Striped Bass" is the major paper in this volume.

Nicholas Karas, *The Complete Book of the Striped Bass* (New York, 1974), is a concise summary of fishing for striped bass in fresh and salt water, and Karas's article, "Catching on to the Newest Fishing Craze," *Outdoor Life*, July 1979, updates freshwater techniques. John N. Cole deals with the plight of stripers in contaminated coastal waters in *Striper* (Boston and Toronto, 1978), while Robert H. Boyle, *The Hudson River* (expanded edition; New York, 1979), discusses striped bass and pollution.

CHAPTER 7

Seth Rosenbaum writes on "Fishing Lures" in *The American Sporting Collector's Handbook* (New York, 1976), edited by Alan J. Liu.

The same book also contains articles by Ted Niemeyer on "Fishing Flies" and Warren Shepard on "Antique Fishing Reels."

CHAPTER 8

For fly-tying techniques, see J. Edson Leonard, *Flies* (New York, 1960), long a standard. A later work, Eric Leiser's *The Complete Book of Fly Tying* (New York, 1977), offers step-by-step directions for tying all types of flies. See also Leiser's *Fly-Tying Materials.* Joe Brook's *Bass Bug Fishing* (New York, 1947), is just what the title says, and the same applies to Joseph D. Bates, Jr., *Streamers & Bucktails* (New York, 1979), an encyclopedic work. Tom Nixon's *Fly Tying and Fly Fishing for Bass and Panfish* (2nd edition, revised; South Brunswick and New York, 1977) has a great deal on bass flies and bugs. Some unusual bass flies and other ties for the advanced tier are offered in *The Fly-Tyer's Almanac* (New York, 1975) and *The Second Fly-Tyer's Almanac* (Philadelphia and New York, 1978), both edited by Robert H. Boyle and Dave Whitlock.

Jigs are dealt with in Lacey E. Gee's and Erwin D. Sias's *How to Fish with Jigs* (Independence, Iowa; 1970) and by that late master of jigging Al Reinfelder in *Bait Tail Fishing* (South Brunswick and New York, 1969).

Index